If More Walls Could Talk

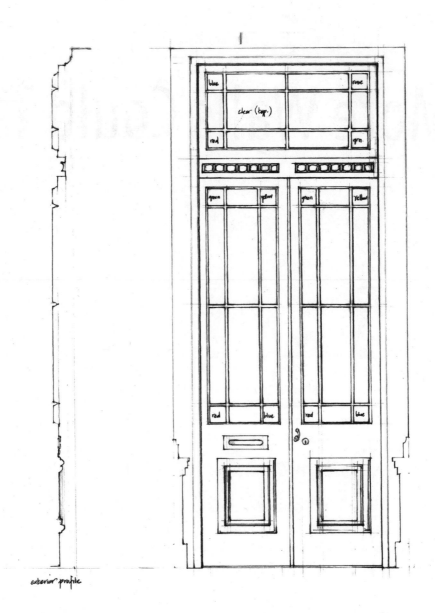

exterior profile

If More Walls Could Talk

Vancouver Island's Houses From the Past

Valerie Green

Illustrated by Lynn Gordon-Findlay

TOUCHWOOD EDITIONS

TouchWood Editions Ltd.
Victoria, BC, Canada
http://www.touchwoodeditions.com
This book is distributed by Heritage House Publishing Co. Ltd., #108-17665 66A Avenue, Surrey, BC, Canada, V3S 2A7.

Cover drawing: Lynn Gordon-Findlay
Book design and layout: Nancy St.Gelais
This book is set in Adobe Garamond Pro.

TouchWood Editions acknowledges the financial support for its publishing program from The Canada Council for the Arts, the Government of Canada through the Book Publishing Industry Development Program (BPIDP) and the Province of British Columbia through the British Columbia Arts Council.

Library and Archives Canada Cataloguing in Publication
Green, Valerie, 1940-
    If more walls could talk: Vancouver Island's houses from the past / Valerie Green; illustrated by Lynn Gordon-Findlay.

    Includes bibliographical references and index.

    ISBN 1-894898-22-2

    1. Historic buildings — British Columbia — Vancouver Island. 2. Dwellings — British Columbia — Vancouver Island. 3. Vancouver Island (B.C.) — History. I.Gordon-Findlay, Lynn, 1960– II. Title.

FC3844.7.B8G74 2004   971.1'2   C2004-905045-1

The Canada Council | Le Conseil des Arts
for the Arts | du Canada

BRITISH
COLUMBIA
ARTS COUNCIL
We acknowledge the support of the Province of British Columbia through the British Columbia Arts Council

This book has been produced on 50% recycled/50% post-consumer recycled paper, processed chlorine free and printed with vegetable-based inks.

CONTENTS

For two "forever" friends —

Shirley in England and Gerri in Canada

Valerie Green

Dear Alissa,

This one is for you!

Lynn Gordon-Findlay

Acknowledgments

Once again I owe sincere thanks to the many people who assisted me in the research for *If More Walls Could Talk.* I would like to acknowledge everyone individually, but the list would be far too long. Instead, I simply offer gratitude to all the current and past owners of each house whose story I have told. There were many of you who offered me hospitality while we discussed your home and talked about its history. Thank you all.

Individual and special thanks to Helen Stewart, Joan Wenman, Ray Webber, Jim Munro, Susan and Patrick Bulmer, Bud and Lyn Collins, David Coulson, Anthea and Darrel Archer, Judy Oliver, Marta Williamson, Jim and Margaret Cadwaladr, Henk and Brenda Witmans, Anne Klees, Mike and Maureen Shipton, Kim Sleno and Brad Wylie.

In addition, my gratitude to all the historical societies, archives and museums throughout Vancouver Island that opened their doors and their hearts to my project. Special thanks to Priscilla Carr at the Cowichan Museum and Archives and to Heather Maloney of the Port Alberni Historical Society, for going above and beyond the call in order to assist me. They made my research much easier.

Thanks also to the people of the North Island, especially Gordie Graham for stories of Telegraph Cove and Louise Smith for those of Port McNeill, and to the editor of the *North Island Gazette*, Mark Allan, who ran a story about my project in order to stir up interest in old homes.

Thanks once again to TouchWood Editions for publishing this sequel to the "Walls project" and for a thorough and meticulous edit. And thank you, Lynn, for adding your magic.

Finally, thanks to my own family, who allowed me the time to visit the past, and especially to David, who accompanied me on many up-island trips in order to track down a house. His patience and understanding were much appreciated in the midst of other family turmoil, and he remains my "rock." David, Matt and Kate have always allowed me to escape into the world of writing — and they have never questioned my need to do that. Thank you, guys. I love you all.

Valerie Green

Introduction

Vancouver Island is known primarily for its pristine beauty, its year-round mild climate and its rich variety of history and legend. The island's history dates back centuries, from the fascinating culture of its First Nations to European settlement in 1843 on its southern tip at Fort Victoria, described by James Douglas as "a perfect Eden."

In spite of this rich history, Vancouver Island is not specifically known for its heritage architecture, except for Victoria, the province's capital city. When European settlers began to arrive in droves, however, from the late 1850s onwards, they built their homes in a manner that attempted to recreate the lifestyles they had lived in their countries of birth. These houses, some of which have survived to this day, are our past, and many of their stories were told in *If These Walls Could Talk.*

Gradually, Vancouver Island's population began to grow. People settled in Duncan and the Cowichan Valley; in the coal-mining town of Nanaimo; in Parksville, Qualicum Beach and Courtenay; on the west coast in Port Alberni; and in Campbell River and the North Island. By the turn of the century, some of the most sought-after architects of the day, such as Samuel Maclure, were designing homes in these areas.

This second volume of stories, *If More Walls Could Talk,* showcases a selection of these homes. Some are grand and some are simple; all are an expression of how those who came before us lived their lives.

Greater Victoria and Southern Vancouver Island

In *If These Walls Could Talk,* 50 heritage homes were explored in the Greater Victoria area, including the municipalities of Saanich, Oak Bay and Esquimalt, and the city itself. In this volume, I have included a few more from this region, as well as notable homes in the Highlands and Western Communities. Once again I found homes of note with enchanting tales from the past.

In the first section of this book, houses of various styles with a diversity of stories are described, ranging from large family mansions to small, isolated cabins, from a house initially built as a ballroom to houses that have been renovated and remodelled, from houses with resident ghosts and bomb shelters to a house once thought to have been occupied by a Japanese consul. And I have included three heritage houses now open to the public: Emily Carr House, Helmcken House and Craigflower Farm.

These first 15 houses are all below the " 'Hat," the Malahat Highway, which, in the next section, will lead to a journey of exploration into heritage homes farther up-island.

Join me as we travel back in time, letting these houses tell their stories from the past — if only their walls could talk.

1

CRAIGMILLAR LODGE

Elegance from a Bygone Era

"Craigmillar Lodge" is a prominent landmark standing majestically at the corner of Kathleen Street and Tattersall Drive in Saanich. It has often been described as one of the grandest houses in that community, and its imposing size and appearance justify that description. Designed by William Jacobus Semeyn in Tudor-Revival style and built by contractor A. H. Mitchell on land once owned by John Work Tolmie, the house was completed in 1913. Its first owners were John and Kate (Fraser) Brown, whose Scottish background led them to give their home its name.

Scotland's Craigmillar Castle had a long and colourful history, going back to the year 1212. It served as a residence for Mary, Queen of Scots and was used for many years by the royal family as an adjunct to Edinburgh Castle and Holyrood House. It was then privately owned for decades and underwent many renovations. During one of these, in 1813, a walled-up skeleton was found. Other than these few facts, the castle's history and that of its residents have always remained very private.

Its namesake lodge on Tattersall Drive has a masonry first floor, half-timbered upper floors and half-hipped gables. The front veranda is a three-storey wing thrusting out beyond the facade, and the arches spanning the veranda openings are duplicated above the central panes of the main-floor windows. One might suppose that such a fashionable home was built for someone of money and importance, but John Brown was a retired Victoria post office worker who simply aspired to elegance. He emigrated to Canada as a young man and lived in Winnipeg before arriving in Victoria in the 1880s.

Kate Brown also owned the Roccabella Boarding House in downtown Victoria, which was run by her brother, John Fraser. Fraser tended the surrounding grounds, while Kate, obviously an industrious woman, operated the Cherry Bank boarding house on Burdett Street. This building had previously been the residence of James Graham Brown, a relative of Kate's husband, but after a wing was added in 1897, it became a guest house.

On the large acreage at Craigmillar Lodge, Kate Brown briefly grew produce for the Cherry Bank's kitchens. By the 1940s, the Cherry Bank had changed hands a few times and a coffee shop had been added; this was the beginning of its transformation into a hotel.

~ 1210 Tattersall Drive ~

During the following years, many military people were residents of the guest house.

By 1954, when more liberal liquor laws were in effect, a cocktail lounge was incorporated into the building, followed by the opening of the famous Spare Rib House in the original dining room; the Cherry Bank's spare ribs were once considered the finest in Canada. Ten years later, however, the hotel was bankrupt. It was then purchased by David and Clair Bowman, who set about injecting new life into Kate Brown's old place by creating an atmosphere of the Gay Nineties in the hotel, while also instituting a nightly singalong under rotating glass-ball chandeliers in what was called the Roaring 20s Lounge. Soon the Cherry Bank was prospering once again. In 1984, David Bowman turned the Roaring 20s into the first lounge in western Canada where Trivial Pursuit could be played. More updating in 1989 further improved the hotel, yet still preserved reminders of bygone days. Sadly, the landmark Cherry Bank is scheduled to be torn down in 2004.

John and Kate Brown did not live to see any of these changes. John passed away in 1913 and Kate in 1916, after which their home on Tattersall Drive was held in trust for a few years. Later owners of Craigmillar Lodge were John Lawrence Pridham, Kate Walkem and the Pollard family, who moved to Victoria from the Orient and owned the property from 1928 until 1952.

In the mid-1950s, the once-regal private residence was divided into 12 apartments, owned for many years by the Giacomo Amarilli family. Because of its grandeur and importance in Saanich, heritage designation was granted to Craigmillar Lodge in 1987. The Amarilli family sold the property in 2001 to Ross and Sharon Meek.

Like its namesake in Scotland, Craigmillar has always kept a private air about it, with owners and occupants who do not seek the limelight. Today, the only reminder of Craigmillar Lodge's original owners is Kathleen Street, named in honour of the hardworking Kate Brown.

HELEN'S HOUSE
Full of Enchanting Myths and Magic

Teacher, writer, printmaker, storyteller and illustrator of children's books, Helen Stewart works in an atmosphere of intrigue and magic at her 1912 heritage home on Tudor Avenue at Ten Mile Point near Cadboro Bay.

She and her family have lived in this delightful house since 1979, and her surroundings have inspired much of her work. The house was built for a man of German descent whose original intention was just to build a large ballroom where his daughter could host dances and parties for her friends. The story told through the decades is that the unnamed German set off one day in his rowboat into the bay and literally "disappeared into the sunset," never to be seen again. He left behind his ballroom, which by then included a small upstairs area, and all its contents.

The abandoned building was then supposed to become an orphanage for English children who were due to sail to Canada during World War I. However, between February and September of 1915, some 50 ships, including the ill-fated liner *Lusitania,* were hit by German submarines. It is assumed that the English orphans were either aboard one of those vessels or, because of the inherent danger on the high seas, never left England at all. The house on Tudor Avenue was then designated as a hospital for wounded war veterans, and still more bedrooms were built upstairs.

Stories abound about subsequent owners through the years, and fact and fiction become entwined. One family decided to paint the floors black and all the walls red, giving rise to a rumour that the house was used as a gambling den and that liquor was being brought in from notorious Smugglers' Cove nearby. This story, although intriguing and colourful, was later refuted.

Following World War II, the building again reverted to a hospital, and myths and legends arose concerning the occupants. A shooting is said to have occurred in the ballroom, and someone purportedly had a leg amputated there. In addition, a resident ghost began to make an appearance; this might have been the long-lost German, disapproving of some of the goings-on in his ballroom. What is known for certain, however, is that military officers occupied the house during the war, and a later occupant of the house was a well-known portrait artist.

Since Helen Stewart has taken over ownership, she has used the old ballroom as a workplace to create

— 2875 Tudor Avenue —

her books and prints, and to display works of art. The spacious former ballroom certainly lends itself to such creativity. Helen does not dispute the existence of a ghost in the house, since strange things have occurred during her occupancy. For example, one particular closet always emitted "bad vibes" until she gave it a thorough cleaning, so she is reluctant to dismiss entirely the existence of a ghostly presence.

For further inspiration, she has transformed her garden into a mini-Butchart Gardens, which has led to her participation in the annual Victoria Conservatory Garden Tour. She also does fundraising projects, gives talks to schoolchildren on book production and offers printmaking demonstrations to groups. Her "ballroom studio" has also been featured in two annual Cadboro Bay Artists' Studio Tours. Her children's books, *Christmas Snowflake, The Porcelain Doll* and *A Child's Enchanted Garden* all reflect the curious historical influences surrounding her, be they fact, fiction or pure fantasy.

Born in Rochester, New York, Helen moved with her family in 1946 to Berkeley, California, where she grew up and was educated. Her mother was a civil-rights activist who frequently took the teenaged Helen to Martin Luther King, Jr., rallies. Helen felt greatly privileged to have heard King's renowned "I Have a Dream" speech.

When she was 21 she married and moved to McBride, in northern British Columbia, to live on a sheep farm in a Mennonite community. This was a major culture shock for her, but the lifestyle taught her to be self-reliant on the farm while her husband was away at university. She quickly learned a great deal about sheep and how to cope with the constant threat of nearby predators such as bears and coyotes, at the same time managing to raise her five children. She has recently written about those experiences in her latest book *Berkeley to the Barnyard — A Far Cry From Home.*

Helen's rich and varied past and her present colourful surroundings have served her well, enhancing her talents, and her house on Tudor Avenue continues to abound with myths and magic.

MIRAMAR

The Evolution of a Stylish House

Designed by architect Percy Leonard James, "Miramar" on Seaview Road at Ten Mile Point is a handsome building that has changed considerably over the years.

The house was built in 1927 for Cecil and Verna Branson. Cecil was president of Branson, Brown & Company, a firm dealing in stocks, bonds, real estate and insurance. The original design, although primarily in the traditional Arts and Crafts style, also incorporated Tudor-Revival details. The outside walls and gabled dormers were clad in stucco and half-timbering, and the roof was cedar-shingled. Several large, arched windows were built into the design, and the brick chimneys each comprised two diamond-shaped stacks. The view of the house from the water was far grander than the view from the road, which gave it an unfinished appearance. Unfortunately, Branson lost a great deal of his money in the 1929 stock-market crash and the Bransons eventually left Victoria.

By 1936, the property was owned by Marian and Victor Sherman. Marian was the oldest of eight children of Hewitt Bostock, a distinguished British Columbia senator; she had come to Victoria as a child with her parents in 1894. The Bostock family home was east of Moss Street on Rockland Avenue, and was better known in later years as the Caroline Macklem Home. The Bostocks named their home "Schuhuum," an Aboriginal word meaning "windy place," and it was there that Marian lived during her childhood. The family also spent time on their ranch near Kamloops.

At the age of 15, Marian was sent to school in England, and later she became a medical student at St. George's Hospital in London. She obtained her medical degree at the London School of Medicine, and during World War I was appointed house surgeon at St. George's, a considerable distinction for a woman at that time.

By 1922, Marian was doing missionary work in India and it was there that she met her future husband, Victor Sherman, who worked for the Imperial Bank of India. The Shermans remained in India until 1934, after which they retired and eventually took up residence at the Ten Mile Point home in Victoria in 1936.

Although Marian Sherman never actually practised medicine in Canada, she devoted the next 40 years of her life to many worthwhile humanitarian and medical

— 2901 Seaview Road —

causes. Her strong views about life and religion, and her undying devotion to such causes as mental health and pro-choice abortion rights, often earned her the reputation of an eccentric. She thought that the world would be a far better place with fewer leaders and more peacemakers. Her outspokenness and controversial opinions at that time generated criticism, but she always welcomed it. She was once quoted as saying: "I don't mind what others think, if I can only get them to read more and think more. Don't you think the art of conversation could do with a little promotion?"

Marian Sherman was definitely a woman with a mission in life. She was a pioneer and pathfinder who founded the Humanist League of Canada. In 1950, she became chairperson of the mental-hygiene committee for the Canadian Council of Women. Shortly before her death in August 1975, she was named Canadian Humanist of the Year. Many prominent Victorians gathered to honour her at her memorial service. The original Miramar, the Shermans' family home, was indeed a fitting monument to an incredible woman. The house remained family-owned until 1984, when it was purchased by the Imperial Bank of India and rented out for a while.

In 1993, J. and K. Pullen became the new owners, and they soon began a major restoration job on the building. According to heritage groups at the time, the Pullens' initial plans involved "doubling the size of the existing structure and would change the setting and historical significance, and the relative[ly] modest dwelling would be transformed into a mansion that would bear little resemblance to the original Percy Leonard James design."

Other opinions were considered as the Pullens' proposal was reviewed. The renovations finally went ahead, but today's structure, although a splendid seafront mansion, does bear little resemblance to James's original Miramar, so revered by heritage experts.

Comparing the old with the new, one cannot help but wonder whether such major alterations to a heritage home are a good idea, since the original features have now been lost. The Pullens, however, still retain a keen interest in the history of their fine home.

BAY BREEZE MANOR

The Restoration of Ira Wilson's House

Ira Wilson was one of the first people to farm in the Cadboro Bay area of Saanich. His name appears on voters' lists as far back as 1875, and by 1882 he had purchased 60 acres of land and was farming in earnest.

In 1890, he built his delightful Queen Anne-style farmhouse on Telegraph Bay Road. Although a long-established member of the community, little is known about him. His wife was Ruth Evans, the daughter of Benjamin Evans, one-time owner of the Wot Cheer House on Yates Street, which later became the Dominion Hotel.

Much more is known about Wilson's Welsh father-in-law, Benjamin Evans, a man who was tough but fair in his dealings with the local First Nations. He was the first European farmer in the Mystic Spring area of southwest Cadboro Bay. Slight of build, Evans gained a reputation as a well-respected man who could easily hold his own in the wilderness. Later in life, he was appointed an usher of the Supreme Court of B.C. and, as such, became a close friend and confidant of the famous Judge Matthew Begbie, often accompanying him on journeys through the Cariboo. The judge even left a small legacy to Benjamin Evans in his will.

While Ira and Ruth Wilson were farming in Cadboro Bay, Ira also worked for Robert Rithet at his Broadmead farm. When an explosion occurred at the Giant Powder Works at Ten Mile Point in the late 1880s, A. E. Morris (later of Government Street tobacco-store fame) was injured, and it was Ira Wilson's hay wagon that acted as the ambulance, carrying Morris to St. Joseph's Hospital so that he could receive speedy medical attention for his severe burns. Wilson was credited with saving Morris' life; this is one of the few incidents ever reported about the Wilsons' farming days in Cadboro Bay. Only 42 years old when he died in 1892, Ira Wilson was buried in Ross Bay Cemetery, and Wilson Street in Esquimalt is named for him.

The farmhouse had numerous owners in the following years, including an Englishman, Frederick William Blankenbach, who occupied it from 1900 to 1906. Blankenbach was a pioneer of the Turtle Mountain district in Manitoba before he moved to Victoria in 1900. He held numerous important posts with the Anglican Synod of the Diocese of British Columbia, including that of lay secretary from 1909 to 1943, honourable treasurer of the provincial synod from 1935 to 1938,

~ 3930 Telegraph Bay Road ~

and secretary of Christ Church Cathedral Buildings Limited from 1922 to 1947. The Blankenbach family named the house "Westward Ho."

After Blankenbach left, ownership of the farmhouse changed frequently. At one time, it was used as a rooming house, and suffered considerable neglect. Since 1998, however, the farmhouse, now renamed "Bay Breeze Manor," has been owned by Max and Janet Andersen, who have devoted much time to renovating and remodelling in order to recapture the heritage value of Wilson's old farmhouse. The Andersens used archival photographs as a guide when restoring and replacing various pieces of the original historic trim.

They also stripped the interior of the house down to the baseboards and repainted it in attractive tones, according to advice from heritage experts. Max did much of the carpentry work himself while Janet designed the layout and chose the colour. New flooring of old-growth fir throughout helps convey the character of a former era. The surrounding gardens have also been restored.

Ira Wilson's farmhouse is now run as the Bay Breeze Manor Bed & Breakfast, in conjunction with the Andersens' other bed & breakfast on Kingston Street in Victoria, Andersen Manor. The work they devoted to the Wilsons' old home on Telegraph Bay Road earned them a well-deserved Hallmark Society Award of Merit in May 2001.

If Ira Wilson were able to see his house today, he would no doubt be delighted. It is a fine example of what dedicated heritage restorers can achieve with a little imagination and a lot of hard work.

ACRYSE

The Wenmans' House in the Woods

Tucked away down a long, narrow lane in Gordon Head is a charming house built in 1913 for John and Alice Wenman. The house is surrounded by numerous trees, many of which are of heritage value, and was appropriately named "Acryse," meaning "clearing in the woods." This Old-English word is of Kentish derivation, which is appropriate as the Wenmans originally came from Kent, England. Ninety years later Acryse is still Wenman-owned.

The house was built by contractor Edward Merrett in a prairie-style design with arches and full-length wooden verandas. When the roof was redone recently, four previous layers of roofing were found underneath. The intriguing chimneys were rebuilt a few years ago by craftsman Willie Tobler, using heritage bricks from a building which stood long ago where Victoria's Mayfair Mall is today.

The house is now owned by Joan Wenman, granddaughter of the original owners. She is proud of her grandfather's home and aims to retain its unique heritage features. Her grandfather's parents came from England to Toronto, where they homesteaded around 1870 before moving to Manitoba and settling in Souris, where the soil was thought to be much better. It was in Souris that John Wenman met and married Alice.

Soon after their marriage they moved to England because Alice did not take to the farming life, but in 1912 the couple returned to Canada, this time to Victoria, which boasted a more English lifestyle. In these more civilized circumstances, they raised two sons, Reginald and Godfrey.

The Gordon Head area at that time was at the height of a real-estate boom and the Wenmans purchased 10 acres of land for $2,000 an acre from a Mr. Norman. They then built Acryse on their acreage at a cost of approximately $8,000 and lived in a small cottage on the property while the house was being constructed. Like many others in the neighbourhood, John Wenman set about growing strawberries and daffodils, but he was considered more of a gentleman farmer. He was nonetheless able to make a good living for his family in the countryside.

His greatest passion in life, however, was the game of cricket, and it was in the sporting world that the name Wenman became well known. Both the Wenman

~ 2144 Wenman Road ~

sons played cricket, and Godfrey was later involved in promoting the game of rugby in Victoria.

Reginald Wenman married Evelyn Lytton, daughter of Claude Lytton, assistant land agent for 37 years for the Esquimalt & Nanaimo Railway. Lytton had come to Victoria in 1908 after serving for 10 years in the British Imperial Army in Hong Kong, Singapore and India. His musical talents led to his first job in Victoria, playing at the grand opening of the Empress Hotel in 1908. In 1912, he had a home built on Ernest Avenue in Victoria, also by contractor Edward Merrett, and called it "Oakdale."

As a boy, Reginald attended the University School (now called St. Michael's University School) and he later taught there for some 46 years. He retired from teaching in 1971, but the Wenman connection with St. Michael's has continued, with subsequent generations also attending the school.

Both Reginald and Godfrey had fond recollections of growing up in Gordon Head. They recalled having to walk the three miles from their home to attend St. Luke's Church on Cedar Hill Cross Road and the rare excursions into town by horse and buggy. Winters were always somewhat bleak out in the countryside, especially so the winter of 1916, often referred to as "the Year of the Big Snow." One small store, standing at the corner of Tyndall and San Juan and run by a Mrs. Sadler, served the entire neighbourhood.

In 1946, John Wenman subdivided half of his property and in 1955, Reginald and Godfrey subdivided the remainder. Today the Wenman home sits on the remaining two acres.

The foundation and veranda posts are said to be made of pig-granite found on the land. This may have been an inferior type of granite, hence "pig," or possibly the expression was derived from the word pegmatite. All the masonry is the work of Richard Williams. A dormer above the main entrance has been enclosed to form a delightful room with magnificent views across the property toward the water and beyond. All of Edward Merrett's original ledgers detailing the costs, time spent and subcontractors used for the building of Acryse still exist in archival records.

Joan Wenman, who lives and works in Vancouver, has rented out the house for a number of years. When she retires, she plans to return to her old family home in the woods.

TIGARA

The Alaska Connection

Just at the point where Gordon Head Road curves to become Ferndale Road sits a house with a remarkably interesting history. Its name, "Tigara," comes from an Inuit word meaning "the point."

Around 1900, this entire area was settled by real-estate agent Frederick Appleton, who in 1910 set about subdividing his property into lots of two acres or more. This was the first such subdivision to occur in Gordon Head for residential purposes. Appleton built two houses on his land, first a small cottage and then a much larger house; the larger was moved about a hundred yards in 1925 to its present location and then renovated by local builder Wilfred Melhuish for new owner Peter Trimble Rowe. Rowe, a native of Toronto, had purchased the house and 10 adjoining acres for $16,500.

Rowe was born in 1856 and trained for the ministry at Trinity College, Toronto. While working near Sault Ste. Marie, Ontario, he was approached by the American Episcopal Church to establish a mission in Sitka, Alaska.

He readily agreed, and in 1898 he was elected the first Episcopal bishop of Alaska, a position he held until his death in 1941. During those years, he and his family divided their time between Alaska and the Gordon Head Road house in Saanich, which they named "Tigara." Rowe himself remained in Alaska for most of that time, returning home to his family a few times each year and telling fascinating, colourful stories about establishing the mission. Rowe had first headed north in 1895 and had witnessed the hectic days of the Klondike Gold Rush of 1897 and 1898. Bishop Rowe was one of the first men of the cloth to visit the mining camps in that vast territory.

The house was renamed "Netherby" by the third owners, the Reid family. During their occupancy, duroid shingles were placed over the original clapboard siding, but many of the other features remained intact.

In the early 1990s, the house was purchased by its fourth owners, Susan and Patrick Bulmer who, over the past dozen years, have made many alterations to the house both inside and out. A new interior staircase and outside veranda have been added, but by far their greatest accomplishment was the garden summer house that now stands on their grounds. This building has a history of its own and has turned into a major achievement and success story on the part of the Bulmers.

~ 4305 Gordon Head Road ~

The summer house originally formed part of Colonel Alan Sharland's estate on Arbutus Road in Gordon Head. That estate itself was once part of a parcel of land that was bought in 1858 by Joseph McKay, a chief trader with the Hudson's Bay Company. In 1872 he sold 296 acres of this land, a tract that stretched from Arbutus Road north to the sea and from Haro Road to Telegraph Bay Road, to George Janes. Janes cleared the land, cutting and hauling cordwood until around 1914, when he left the area. He did, however, retain the land until 1927, at which time he sold 207 acres to the Queenswood Land Company. A portion went to Colonel Sharland, who set about building a most elaborate English-style mansion, for which he spared no expense.

The grounds of Sharland's Queenswood House were equally elaborate and, among other things, contained a garage, chauffeur's quarters, a tennis court, a greenhouse and the summer house. When the Sharlands had to sell this beautiful property and return to England, the house and grounds were purchased by the Kilgour family, who also ran the Birdcage Restaurant on Government Street in Victoria.

In the 1950s, a large fire occurred at Queenswood House, causing a great deal of damage that would have meant major repair work and financial investment, so four years later the whole estate was put up for sale. The mansion itself was eventually demolished to allow the Sisters of St. Ann to complete in 1967 their new house of studies and residence, which they now run as an inter-denominational retreat.

But what of the elusive summer house? The Bulmers had long admired it, and during the 1990s they asked for permission to move it to the grounds of their home on Gordon Head Road, which by then they had rechristened Tigara.

So it was that in the summer of 1998 Patrick Bulmer began to take the summer house apart piece by piece and transport the whole thing to his property. He then lovingly and painstakingly rebuilt and restored it to its original look, adding rock work in front and replacing some of the wood that had become infested with carpenter ants. It now sits facing his lawn, framed by trees and shrubbery, just as it once did while gracing the lawns of Queenswood House. Curiously, one of the trees growing alongside it is a Monterey cypress; an identical tree had grown next to it at the Queenswood estate. In July 1999, the newly situated summer house became the perfect setting for the Bulmers' daughter's wedding.

The grounds of Tigara have also become a part of The Land Conservancy's annual house tour, which has attracted as many as 700 visitors.

MOODY HOUSE

A St. Charles Street Treasure Trove

On Sunday, November 4, 2001, a ceremony was held in North Vancouver to unveil a new interpretive walk and playground at Moodyville Park. The ceremony was attended by many dignitaries including the mayor, members of council, local historians and members of the Heritage Advisory Commission.

The most important person there that day, however, was 92-year-old Jean Greenwood. Greenwood was the granddaughter of Sewell Prescott Moody, who established the first European settlement on the north shore, known as Moodyville, in 1863; it grew into the most prosperous settlement on Burrard Inlet. Interestingly, the ceremony in North Vancouver has a strong connection with a house on St. Charles Street in Victoria.

The house, Number 1020, was built around 1900 by Jean's father, Sewell Prescott Moody, Jr., and she and her brother and sister were all born in the house and spent part of their childhood there. Sewell Prescott Moody, Jr., was also born in Victoria; his pioneering father perished at sea in 1875 when the boy was only a year old. The younger Moody worked as a salesman for Simon Leiser, a well-known wholesale merchant in the city. He was married in June 1898 and for the next two years he and his wife, Matilda, lived on Foul Bay Road with Sewell's grandmother, Mrs. Adam Watson, while their house was being built on St. Charles. Their son was born there in 1902 and was followed by two daughters, Clare and Jean. Jean was born in 1909.

The Moodys lived at 1020 St. Charles Street for approximately 18 years. During that time, a few minor alterations were made to the house, which had originally been constructed as a simple west-coast farmhouse with a turret on one corner. They had the house raised in order to install a coal furnace and built a sunroom above what had been the old woodshed. Originally that space was a loft and the Moody children admit to having smoked their first cigarettes up there.

Mr. Moody loved cars and was a friend of automobile pioneer and better-roads promoter Bert Todd, who lived on Linden Avenue. They were two of the first men to have automobiles in the city and belonged to the Victoria Automobile Club; Moody accompanied Todd on many of his pioneering road trips throughout the Pacific Northwest. Moody's intention was to run a Victoria outlet of the Begg Motor Company, which sold

~ 1020 St. Charles Street ~

Cadillacs (one of which he always drove), but the onset of World War I unfortunately stalled his plans.

In May 1915, after the sinking of the *Lusitania,* there was a great deal of anti-German feeling in the city, which resulted in rioting, looting and vandalism against property belonging to people from that country. The Leiser family, who were of German descent, lived opposite the Moodys on St. Charles and were their friends. The Leisers feared the angry mob in town would eventually march up Fort Street and reach their house. The Moodys, therefore, suggested the Leisers bring all their jewellery over to Number 1020, where it would be stored safely in a closet under the stairs.

This was the closet in which Prescott Moody stored his liquor supply, and his daughters recalled in later life how one of their maids, who always enjoyed an afternoon cup of tea, poured only from a certain teapot. Because of a strong smell of liquor on her breath after tea, the family suspected that the teapot did not always contain what it was supposed to and concluded that the tea was probably mixed with some whisky rifled from that same closet under the stairs.

Moody died in 1949 at the age of 75, by which time the family had long since left St. Charles Street and were living in Brentwood Bay, where he had acquired property. He was listed in a 1948 city directory as owning Moody & Riddle, a real estate-and-insurance company.

After the Moodys left 1020 St. Charles, the property was owned briefly by Herbert Middleton, a chief accountant from Shanghai, China, but in May 1921, George Herbert Dawson, the 10th surveyor-general of British Columbia, moved in. Dawson had retired to Victoria in 1917, and had first lived at 1162 Fort Street. Dawson renovated the St. Charles house by extending it on the north side and adding a conservatory on the south. He lived there until his death in 1941, although records show that during the late 1940s and early 1950s the property was in the name of Miss Mary F. Dawson, George's sister.

In the mid-1950s, the house was acquired by Helen and Harold V. Hummel, who renovated the house and turned it into a duplex in 1956. Hummel was an audit accountant with the British Columbia government. After his death, the house remained in his widow's name until her remarriage in the early 1960s to an English lawyer. The title to the house was then put in her new name, Helen Houghton-Beckford.

In 1973 the house was purchased by Mr. and Mrs. Ray Webber, who had been drawn to it from the moment they first saw it. They rented it out for a while before moving in themselves in 1976. Knowing little about the history of the house at that time, the Webbers were in Vancouver visiting a museum when suddenly they spotted an old archival photograph which Mrs. Webber immediately appeared to recognize.

"That's the man I saw standing in the doorway at our house one day," she declared. Her husband, knowing her psychic powers were often correct, did not dispute her claim. She often had visions of things past or premonitions about coming events. On this particular occasion, the photograph she recognized turned out to be that of Sewell Prescott Moody, Junior, who had of course lived in the house but had died many years earlier. They believed they knew then why some mystical impulse had drawn them to buy the house. Mrs. Webber felt a strong connection to the Moody family, and through the years Ray Webber has kept in touch with Moody descendants.

In 2001, Webber sold the house, but he still lives nearby on St. Charles Street. The new owners hope to remodel Number 1020 once again; they plan to attach the house to the neighbouring building in order to create an extended-care home for seniors.

ASHTON

The Evolution of a Rattenbury House

Often described as one of Francis Rattenbury's most powerful architectural statements, the house known as "Ashton" at 1745 Rockland Avenue was built in 1900 for an Ontario lawyer named Lyman Duff.

Duff, the son of a clergyman, arrived in Victoria in 1895 and later opened what would become one of British Columbia's most prestigious law firms. Duff had many friends in high places, such as Sir Wilfrid Laurier, and was later appointed to the B.C. Supreme Court. Eventually he moved on to the Supreme Court of Canada to become Canada's chief justice in the 1930s; he was knighted by King George V.

Lyman Duff had hired Rattenbury to design a home on Rockland Avenue at a time when Rattenbury was experimenting with the Chateau style on many of his residential buildings. Ashton's curious pointed dormers and bays and its sweeping shingled facade are marks of this style. Behind its granite pillars, Ashton was destined to become one of the foremost landmarks on Rockland Avenue.

An amusing story is told of when the house was first completed and ready for occupancy. The Duffs decided to celebrate by holding a party, little realizing that Rattenbury had encountered problems with some of his subcontractors. Consequently, the plumbing had not been hooked up in the downstairs bathroom. During the party, many guests used that bathroom, which unfortunately caused the pipes to overflow and flood the Chinese house servant's room below. It was not a very auspicious beginning.

After Duff left B.C. and went back to Ontario and an even more prestigious career, James Albert Lindsay took up residence at Ashton in 1912.

During the Depression, Dr. Alvin Gray purchased Ashton for $5,000. The Grays, who had four daughters, were involved in the world of music, and the house was often the venue for receptions and musical events. Dr. Gray was also active with the St. John's Ambulance organization, in which he served as a knight commander. Many well-known and important Victorians were entertained at the house during those years.

During World War II, Dr. Gray was heavily involved in civil defence, and perhaps because of this role and his duties with the St. John's Ambulance, he became somewhat obsessed with safety issues in the event that Canada were ever invaded. With this in mind, he had

~ 1745 Rockland Avenue ~

25

the first of three bomb shelters built at Ashton. The first, which had already formed part of the basement, was now reinforced with beams 12 inches thick and 12 feet long. The second was built in the backyard and was used primarily for storage, with trapdoors leading to an underground pit. The third was built much later as an atomic-bomb shelter during the Cold War. A hollow was dug out where the garden pond had been, and the shelter was bulit there and then stacked with supplies of food and water; today a tennis court covers it.

The Grays left Ashton in the early 1960s, and the George Jones family took up residency there. In 1970, Jack Mears and his wife bought the house and remodelled it, adding a glassed-in back veranda and a new kitchen with an adjoining family room.

Ashton's evolution through the years has taken many twists and turns, but the home remains in prime condition and is still a landmark on Rockland Avenue.

NEWHOLM

An Intriguing House of Early Scandals

The story of "Newholm" at 1648 Rockland Avenue begins with Henry M. Dumbleton, who was born in South Africa and arrived in Oregon in 1888 with his parents. By 1892 he had moved to Victoria. Before settling in this part of the world, however, he had already seen a great deal of the British Empire and during his young days had been involved in the Zulu War. He had also accumulated a great deal of money.

Dumbleton inherited a love for the outdoors and hunting in the land of his birth, and once in Canada he used his wealth to buy extensive acreage in the Rockland area. He lived in a large home on Rockland Avenue (then known as Belcher Avenue) which he called "Rocklands." It is believed that Rockland Avenue was named after that home. He also purchased nearly 700 acres in the Highlands near Pike Lake, which he used for hunting and the establishment of a farm.

In 1897 he commissioned Francis Rattenbury to design a home near his own in what was then known as the Rockland Estates. This house was for his son, Alan Southey Dumbleton, who named it "Newholm." It still stands today and is currently the home of Victoria bookstore owner Jim Munro and his wife, artist Carole Sabiston.

Alan Dumbleton was called to the bar on June 8, 1893, and according to historian Harry Gregson in *A History of Victoria, 1842–1970,* later had to "leave Victoria after litigation was brought against him involving his handling of trust funds for a number of very prominent Victoria families." The whole affair caused a scandal in the city and cast the Dumbleton family in a bad light.

However, while practising law at 531 Bastion Square, Alan Dumbleton enjoyed his home on Rockland Avenue, which Rattenbury had designed in simplified Queen Anne, Arts and Crafts and Tudor styles. Dumbleton eventually returned to Victoria and, by 1909, had moved to "Fairoaks" on Cloverdale Avenue. By 1920 he was a resident of the Highland Lake area, where his uncle, Charles Dumbleton, and a cousin, Percy, were also living. The Dumbletons still owned a fair amount of land there, but most had been purchased by the Todd family. For many years the Todds attempted to buy out the Dumbletons. Eventually, about 18 years after the end of World War II, they succeeded, buying the remaining Dumbleton property for $16,000, thereby owning the entire acreage around Pike Lake.

~ 1648 Rockland Avenue ~

In September 1911, 1648 Rockland was purchased by another lawyer, Malcolm Bruce Jackson, for $7,500, and shortly afterward it became the centre of a second scandal. Jackson began his law career studying with Colin H. Campbell in Manitoba and later with George William Allan. In 1896 he was called to the Queen's Bench as an attorney in Manitoba, before moving to British Columbia in the early years of the 20th century to practise law there.

Jackson lived in the house on Rockland for a number of years and his law career was comparatively uneventful until he was asked to assist a friend on a Vancouver murder case. His friend was Attorney General Alexander Manson, and the case in question was the unsolved murder of Janet Smith, a young Scottish housemaid who had worked for a prominent Vancouver family and was found dead in the basement of their house.

The case had reached a stalemate when Jackson was called upon in late 1924. The United Council of Scottish Societies was delighted that someone else was finally taking an interest in the case, which it believed had been brushed aside by investigators until then. However, the police were not happy when Jackson began digging around in their territory.

Numerous mistakes and oversights had been made in the initial investigation. As a result the case, which was at first considered a possible suicide, continued on the premise that Wong Foon Sing, the Chinese houseboy who had discovered the body, might also have been the perpetrator of the crime. Pressure was placed upon the authorities to make an arrest. Attorney General Manson, along with many others at that time, was known to have an intense hatred for Oriental people, but the bungled investigation offered no proof of what had really happened. Many other rumours circulated, including the possible involvement of a drug-smuggling ring and an equally shocking suspicion that the unfortunate housemaid had been caught in the middle of a lovers' quarrel between Jack Nichol, the son of then-Lieutenant-Governor W. G. Nichol, and his fiancée, Lucille McRae, daughter of multi-millionaire A. D. McRae. Another disturbing rumour was that poor Miss Smith had been raped and killed by a member of Vancouver's high society.

Manson decided to call in Inspector Cruickshank of the B.C. Provincial Police to take over the case from the Point Grey police. Cruickshank then hired other detectives to help with the investigations. When Jackson was brought in, he landed right in the middle of the somewhat suspect police investigation that had led to Janet Smith's body being exhumed on August 28 that year. A second autopsy revealed no further clues.

When Wong was later kidnapped by persons unknown and subjected to intensive torture for 42 days, the story took on a completely different light. It was now seen as a case of racial bigotry and many people in authority, including Manson himself, were suspected of involvement in the kidnapping and torture. A dark cloud was also cast over anyone connected with Manson, including Malcolm Jackson.

Wong was eventually found, but the public was outraged by the way he had been treated. Manson, who had probably known of the kidnapping, tried to distance himself from the events. Eventually Wong was arrested and awaited trial, but still no evidence linked him to the murder. On June 17, 1925, Oscar and William Robinson and Varity Norton, all employed by the Canadian Detective Bureau, were arrested for his kidnapping. Eight more summonses were issued, four of which were for officers with the Point Grey police force.

This entire tragic episode in the B.C. justice system left behind a trail of disasters. A young girl had been murdered and the case was never solved; racial bigotry had raised its ugly head, causing an innocent man to be prejudged and tortured; rumours of illicit happenings in high places had run rampant; a drug-smuggling ring had been uncovered and suspicion hung over the head of Janet Smith's employer, F. L. Baker, an exporter of pharmaceutical drugs; and Attorney General Manson's career had been destroyed and he and his colleagues, including Jackson, were all sharply criticized.

Wong was never sent to trial and was eventually released. In March 1926 he decided to return to China. Today Janet Smith's ghost is believed to haunt the house in which she was murdered, perhaps searching for the justice she never received in her lifetime.

Malcolm Jackson continued to live in the Rockland

Avenue house until his death in 1947. By the 1950s, Newholm was owned by the Walker family. Later owners were P. G. Keogh, N. L. Ross and F. M. Mandall, from whom Jim Munro and his first wife, author Alice Munro, purchased the house in 1966.

Munro moved to Victoria in 1963 and set up a long, narrow bookstore on Yates Street in the area of the movie theatres. His stock consisted mainly of paperbacks at a time when only hardcover books were considered "appropriate" books to own. His main competitors were the book departments at The Bay and Eaton's, but soon Munro had built up a loyal clientele who followed him to his larger premises on Fort Street in 1979 and then to his current location on Government Street in 1984. Eight weeks after purchasing that building, he set about restoring it to the former neoclassical design of architect Thomas Hooper. Munro also had his house on Rockland Avenue to work on. Newholm had fallen into a sad state of repair and needed major alterations. Previous owners had divided it into suites, so the first job was to convert it back to a single-family home. Jim believes he wanted to own the house because he had what he describes as "visions of grandeur" after first seeing it. He managed to scrape together enough money to purchase it at a time when it was difficult to negotiate mortgages. The grounds were also run down, so much work was involved when they finally moved in.

Jim and Alice Munro divorced in 1974 and two years later Jim married Carole Sabiston. Since then a new veranda in the style of Rattenbury's other houses has been built onto the house, and a garage with cupola and weather vane added. Carole works in an attached studio, and her incredible artistic touch is seen throughout the house in the many fabric wall hangings. She has also completely redesigned the grounds.

Today, Newholm is an attractive home that reflects its past grandeur. If its walls could talk, they would no doubt tell us how happy the house is to have outlived its earlier scandals.

EMILY'S HOUSE

"Everything about it was extremely English"
—Emily Carr

The Emily Carr House in Victoria, now a public heritage site, stands at 207 Government Street. It is the birthplace of one of Canada's most famous artists and authors.

Emily's father, Richard, left England as a lad of 19 to see the world. He took part in the California gold rush, but returned to England to get married. He then brought his bride back to California but, according to his daughter Emily, soon discovered he did not like living under any flag other than his own. Though he returned to England, Richard Carr refused to give up his dream of a new land where he could find a better life for his family. Once again he set off with his wife and two small daughters, Edith ("Dede"), and Clara ("Tallie"), eventually reaching Victoria, which Emily Carr later described as "the most English-tasting bit of all Canada."

In 1863, Carr purchased 10 acres of land, part of the parcel then known as Beckley Farm, which had been conveyed by the Hudson's Bay Company to Colonel R. C. Moody in March 1863. Carr purchased the property from Colonel Moody, but later became involved in a dispute over the exact boundaries of his property. He believed he had been shortchanged by some 37 feet in front of the house he had built on it, which was designed by architect John Wright. The jury favoured Moody, but the Carrs moved in anyway on April 1, 1864. The address then was 44 Carr Street.

Two more daughters, Elizabeth and Alice, were born to the Carrs and then, in December 1871, a few months after British Columbia became a province, Emily arrived. Two infant sons died soon after birth, and one more son, Richard, was born after Emily.

The architecture of the Carr house has been described as both "San Francisco Victorian" and "English Gingerbread." In her *Book of Small* Emily stated:

Our Street was called Carr Street after my Father. We had a very nice house and lovely garden and Carr Street was a very fine street. The dirt road waved up and down and in and out . . . the horses made it that way, zigzagging the carts and carriages through it. The rest of the street was green grass and wild roses . . .

~ 207 Government Street ~

Emily also clearly described the house, which she says was large and well-built of California redwood.

> . . . Everything about it was extremely English . . . There were hawthorn hedges and banks of primroses and cow pastures with shrubberies.

One incident that marred this idyllic setting was Richard Carr's run-in with a certain William Lush, who purchased an acre of land from him and then built a saloon alongside the Carrs' property. Emily described the building as "the horridest saloon in town," because although Lush had promised that his establishment would be respectable, it was soon frequented by sailors from Esquimalt who consumed large amounts of liquor and made an incredible amount of noise. Carr was forced to build a very high fence along his property line to protect his family from the drunken spectacles that occurred regularly at Lush's saloon.

Aside from this, the Carrs integrated well into the community and enjoyed all their other neighbours. They employed a Chinese servant named Bong who took care of their needs, and a Native Indian woman they called Wash Mary who did Mrs. Carr's washing every Monday.

Richard Carr died in 1888 and, since his frail wife had predeceased him, he left his house and property to his eldest daughter, Edith Carr. Emily, still only in her teens, managed to escape her older sister's strict rules by leaving Victoria to study art in San Francisco. She later studied in both Paris and London. During those years, she was said to have suffered a nervous breakdown due to extreme stress, possibly caused by her artistic temperament and having had to make the decision to leave behind the security of home. She did not return to Victoria until 1913.

Meanwhile, the original Beckley Farm had been subdivided into 20 lots. Lots 13 to 20, including the property on which the Carr house stood, were part of Richard Carr's original estate. In 1908 the Carr house address was changed to 207 Government Street, and in 1911 Lot 19 was sold to James Townsley for the sum of $2,400. Lot 13, which had been left to Edith, was passed on to her sister Elizabeth upon Edith's death in 1920. (Elizabeth already owned Lot 14.) Lot 17 became Emily's, Lot 18 belonged to sister Clara, and Lot 20 to sister Alice.

Edith Carr also left the house to her sisters Elizabeth and Alice in 1920. Elizabeth then lived in the house and rented out rooms until her own death in 1936. Sometime during these years, the property was once again subdivided into two lots.

After Elizabeth's death, Alice and Emily became the sole beneficiaries of the estate, and a year later further subdivisions were made. Finally, in 1938, Emily and Alice sold the house to Lena Godfrey, a decision Emily was obviously not happy about, as she was said to have remarked on one occasion that she just wished the house would simply fold up and fly away. That way, no one other than the Carrs would have lived there.

Six months after Lena Godfrey's purchase, a fire occurred at the house and a large portion at the back was destroyed. After the damage was repaired, the house was rented out as a rooming house with approximately 12 rooms.

In 1944 William and Sarah Atema bought the house, and the property remained in their names until April 1964, at which time it was purchased by Member of Parliament David Groos. In 1967, long after Emily had died in 1945 and her works had found world fame, the property was conveyed to the Emily Carr Foundation.

By 1972 the house served as a children's art school and gallery that became known as the Emily Carr Arts Centre. In 1976 the property was registered in the name of the Province of British Columbia and made a heritage site open to the public; in 1979 the government began major restoration work on the house.

Emily bought a house on Simcoe Street with her portion of the inheritance and took in boarders to support herself. She called that house the House of All Sorts.

HELMCKEN HOUSE

The Doctor and the Governor's Daughter

It was the perfect 19th-century love match: a union between a young doctor, the first reputable one to arrive in Victoria, and the daughter of the governor, James Douglas. Dr. John Sebastian Helmcken arrived in Victoria in 1850 to work for the Hudson's Bay Company as the fort's doctor, and before long he spotted Cecilia, Douglas's eldest daughter. He became, in his own words, "more or less captivated" by her. He later described the moment of their first meeting in his *Memoirs*. She was, he wrote, "as active as a little squirrel, and one of the prettiest objects [I] have ever seen."

All of Douglas's five daughters were extremely shy, so the courtship between John and Cecilia was typically Victorian and always chaperoned. They were eventually married on December 27, 1852, and Douglas presented the young couple with land on which to build their first home. The property was beside his own house, which stood between Belleville and Elliott streets, where the Royal British Columbia Museum now stands.

The young couple's house on Elliott Square began as a three-room log house, and the contractor was Gideon Halcrow, a builder, mechanic and crofter who had arrived aboard the *Norman Morison* in 1852 and landed this plum assignment. By all accounts, however, Halcrow was rather slow, and in his *Memoirs* John Helmcken frequently complained about the contractor's tardiness. The young couple had to live temporarily in a house on the corner of Government and Yates streets until theirs was completed.

Eventually, however, they were able to move into Helmcken House and Amelia Douglas, Cecilia's mother, was delighted to have her daughter and son-in-law next door. Family traditions and closeness were important to both the Douglas and Helmcken families through the years.

The little three-room log house soon expanded to accommodate the Helmckens' growing family. There were seven children in all, although only four survived infancy, and Cecilia herself died tragically in 1865 after a bout of pneumonia; she was only 31.

The heartbroken young doctor was left to raise his children alone, a task he appears to have accomplished exceptionally well, at the same time becoming a great statesman by helping to negotiate British Columbia's transition into a Canadian province in 1871. In addition,

~ 675 Belleville Street ~
(Beside the Royal BC Museum)

he carried on a medical practice in Victoria and was highly respected, loved and sought after by his patients.

Helmcken's youngest daughter, Edith Louisa (known as Dolly), was only two years old when her mother died, and the family's housekeepers looked after her when her father was away. She became a favourite of her grandfather, Sir James, and grew up adoring her father.

In 1889 Dolly married Ralph Higgins, whose own father, David, was the first speaker of the legislature and the founder of the *Daily Chronicle,* having previously worked at the *British Colonist,* Victoria's first daily newspaper. Dolly and Ralph shared a love of travel and a passion for music. Soon after their return to Victoria from their travels through Europe, Ralph took up a position at the *Daily Colonist.* Within weeks, however, he became seriously ill, had an emergency operation, and died soon after at the young age of 30.

In 1896 Dolly returned to live with her father at Helmcken House and took care of him for the rest of his life until his death in 1920. During that period, a large addition was made to the house for Dolly, who devoted her life not only to her father, but also to many charitable works. She became treasurer of the Protestant Orphanage Society, and was active in numerous projects connected with the Church of Our Lord.

Dolly lived in Helmcken House until her death at the age of 77 in 1939, and during those years she refused to change anything in the house, believing that everything to do with her father was "sacred." She originally left instructions that upon her own death all of her father's writings were to be destroyed and Helmcken House itself torn down. She could not accept the fact that her family's beloved house might one day be neglected and deteriorate, or that her father's *Memoirs* might fall into the wrong hands.

In 1934, however, soon after W. Kaye Lamb was appointed provincial librarian and archivist, he met Dolly Higgins and they became friends. She shared her father's reminiscences with Mr. Lamb and allowed him to consult the five volumes of manuscripts. He began to realize that Dr. Helmcken's *Memoirs* were a treasure to be preserved for future generations and that to destroy them would be "in a considerable measure to destroy his memory."

Dolly must have given this matter a great deal of thought, because her later will made no mention of destroying the manuscripts written by her father or of tearing down Helmcken House. In fact, today, *The Reminiscences of Doctor John Sebastian Helmcken,* edited by Dorothy Blakey Smith, form an important part of British Columbia's historical library.

After Dolly's death, Mr. Lamb visited Helmcken House, accompanied by the Honourable John Hart, then-minister of finance, and witnessed a miracle. Though additions had been made to the little log house through the years, very little else had been disturbed, and Helmcken House still looked much as it had in 1853. Despite the fact that Dr. Helmcken himself had died almost 20 years earlier, his bedroom appeared as though he had left it only that morning, with his clothes hanging neatly in the cupboard and a shirt for the day ready at hand. The men were both astounded and enchanted by the treasures inside Helmcken House, and negotiations soon began between the government and the Helmcken estate to acquire the house. That acquisition was completed in July 1939.

The outbreak of World War II in September 1939 temporarily delayed plans for turning the house into a heritage site, but by August 1941 Helmcken House was finally opened to the public as an historical museum.

It remains the oldest house in British Columbia still on its original site and open for public viewing, and it gives a fascinating glimpse into life as it was lived long ago. Dr. Helmcken's original 19th-century medical kit is just one of the many amazing artifacts to be seen inside Helmcken House today.

CRAIGFLOWER MANOR

The Hill of Flowers

In May 1854, the Hudson's Bay Company (HBC) transferred four sections of land, each over 600 acres, to the Puget Sound Agricultural Company (PSAC).

The intention was to operate four farms on these acreages and bring in sturdy Englishmen of reliable disposition to work them. These farms were soon established and were named View Field Farm, Constance Cove Farm, Colwood Farm and Craigflower Farm.

Craigflower was situated at the head of the Gorge waterway in an area originally known as Maple Point because of the abundance of maple trees growing there. Kenneth McKenzie, who came from Scotland to farm this land, named his new home "Craigflower," meaning a hill of flowers. He did this to honour the English estate of the same name belonging to Sir Andrew Colvile, the HBC governor.

Setting up these farms to be worked by colonists was the HBC's way of establishing a British claim to Vancouver Island. Craigflower Farm was also extremely important to the livelihood of Fort Victoria itself because, situated as it was on the waterway, it provided not only a sheltered haven for passing boats, but also essential supplies of meat, fresh bread and vegetables for the company men at the fort. The farm was soon exporting produce as far away as Russia, as well as producing supplies for the Royal Navy at Esquimalt.

Kenneth McKenzie, his wife Agnes, their five children, and Agnes's brother and sister had set sail from Scotland in 1852 aboard the *Norman Morison,* bound for the new colony where McKenzie was to take up his position as farm bailiff. According to the diary of Robert Melrose, a carpenter contracted to work for McKenzie for five years, the voyage was fraught with danger, one particular hurricane lasting for four days. Buffeted by fierce gales, their approach to Vancouver Island had been anything but easy. When they arrived, the McKenzies were first offered overcrowded accommodation with other families in a loft inside the fort.

In January 1853, however, James Douglas wrote a letter to the Puget Sound Agricultural Company director stating that:

> Mr. McKenzie has just returned from the place selected for his residence, and is pleased with the spot and the buildings already put up, consisting of one house of 50 feet and two

110 Island Highway

cottages 25 feet in length which he can soon render habitable.

Craigflower Farm was intended to become the most successful of the Puget Sound farms and life at Craigflower Manor appeared to be pleasant for the "Laird" and his family. However, judging from Melrose's diary of events at Craigflower, many of the employees appeared to be disgruntled.

One of McKenzie's daughters reminisced in later life that ". . . we were happy as children to run wild at Craigflower after a restricted nursery life in Scotland." She goes on to describe their life there as carefree, with picnics, riding parties and trips by boat up "the Arm" (the Gorge) to visit the fort.

McKenzie's employees painted a rather different picture. They described their employer as an unpleasant taskmaster. Severely punished for disobedience, some left his employ because of the treatment they received. Many of their complaints are a matter of official record and appear to be true, substantiated by other accounts of labour disputes at Craigflower. Even though Craigflower Farm played a large part in early colonial life and was purported to be successful from that perspective, it never made money for the company and more often than not ran at a loss.

Kenneth McKenzie's contract ended in 1865, by which time the farm was in considerable debt. He was required to pay the HBC the sum of $3,000, and this debt hung over him until his death. Meanwhile, he moved his family to the Lake Hill area, where he became a sheep farmer and appeared to be much happier. He died at the age of 63 in 1874 and his wife, Agnes, lived on at Lake Hill until 1897.

Meanwhile, Craigflower Manor was leased out to a series of tenants after the McKenzies left, and during those years some minor structural alterations were made to the house.

In 1922, the HBC remodelled the manor house considerably as a social centre for its employees. Later the farmhouse was leased again, and then, in 1937, it was sold to a Mr. Christie, who transformed it into an annex to his Discovery Motel. Five bathrooms were installed and many of the rooms were also altered at that time. In 1965 Craigflower Manor was sold to the Thompson family, who later sold it to the government.

On October 16, 1967, Victoria architect Peter Cotton was hired by the deputy provincial secretary and the provincial librarian/archivist to submit proposals for the restoration of Craigflower's farmhouse. His task was to make the building look as it had during the McKenzies' occupancy, and 1860 was chosen as the historical setting.

It was a major undertaking that required a lot of time and money. The projected completion date of March 1968 was subsequently extended to June 1969, when the house finally opened to the general public, with some furnishing still to be completed.

During those two years, Cotton and his restoration team became detectives uncovering the mysteries of the manor house through the aid of photographs, old furnishings and McKenzie's own books, ledgers, and correspondence. They studied chimney structures, floors, ceilings, walls, doors, windows and fireplaces, and consulted newspapers from the pertinent years. The result of all their hard work is an authentic, 19th-century reconstruction, but considerable maintenance must be done regularly to preserve this authenticity.

Meanwhile, Craigflower Manor is open to the public, and the blueprints of Peter Cotton's amazing work are preserved in his collections at the British Columbia Archives.

COLES HOUSE

A Family Mosaic in a Rattenbury Jewel

The imposing residence at 851 Wollaston Street is unusual in many ways, but most especially because it is the only one in Esquimalt designed by the renowned architect Francis Rattenbury. It may well be one of his best examples of the English Arts and Crafts style.

At one time, the main entrance faced Dunsmuir Road and consequently the house itself sported the address of 864 Dunsmuir Road. Wollaston Street was formerly known as Stanley Street but the name was changed in 1918. It takes its name either from Edward Wollaston Lang, RN, a fourth lieutenant aboard the survey ship HMS *Fisgard*, or from a local land surveyor named Frederick Wollaston. Part of the street was home to the Wollaston Street rock quarry in the early 1920s.

In 1907, Arthur Coles, a successful real-estate broker, purchased the land where the house now sits for $1,500 from Henry Croft and his wife, the former Mary Dunsmuir. Croft sold the land in order to pay off some of his debts. Coles and his wife, Ada, then commissioned Rattenbury to build them a mansion on the property. Two years later the property and building were assessed at $8,000.

The mansion has four floors and is rectangular in shape. Many Rattenbury features were incorporated into the house, such as an oriel window on the third floor, unusual curved gable ends on the fourth floor and a two-storey porch supported by large, square posts. In addition, there were many elements of the Tudor-Revival and Queen Anne styles so popular at that time.

The house was ready for the Coles to occupy in 1908. Arthur was then in business with his brother-in-law Sam Matson, a landowner and later the publisher of the *Daily Colonist*. Coles was also reeve of Esquimalt from 1916 to 1919, and he continued to run a very successful real estate and insurance business for many years.

Aside from being in business together, Arthur Coles and Sam Matson were married to sisters, Amy and Ada Galley. Through the years the evolution of this interesting mansion has been entwined with these three family names, along with many other intriguing ones. There are, for instance, early connections with the Dunsmuir family and later ones with the prestigious McBrides, Eastons and Beresfords, who were all at various times owners of the property.

~ 851 Wollaston Street ~

Apparently Coles sold the house to Sam and Ada Matson after just a few years. Other residents have included Captain McGreggor F. MacIntosh, who was an officer of the Princess Patricia's Canadian Light Infantry from 1914 to 1919. He married Peggy McBride, the daughter of Sir Richard McBride, premier of British Columbia. Captain MacIntosh lost his right arm in the battle of the Somme in World War I, and his wife was killed in a small-plane crash in 1955. Doctor P. A. C. Cousland and his wife Vivian (who was also a Matson) were owners at one time, and for a while the house was rented by R. H. Pooley.

Later, the house came into the possession of two fascinating sisters, Kathleen De Lapoer Beresford and Vera St. Thomas Francis Easton, who ran it as an elegant boarding house and entertained naval personnel. Even these two sisters have a connection with previous owners and are part of the family mosaic. Their niece, Cecily, was married to Sam and Ada Matson's son, Herbert. Sadly, Cecily and her daughter Mary were both killed in a bombing raid in London during World War II.

Kathleen Beresford (known as Kitty) was a nurse who married a British officer during the war and was widowed shortly thereafter. Vera (affectionately known as "Puggie" to her friends and family) and her sister were the daughters of a wealthy horse breeder from Charlottesville, Virginia, and their mother was from an ancient Norman family.

The sisters grew up in Newmarket, England, with their four siblings and had led an elegant lifestyle which involved travel, governesses and mixing with the cream of society, but when their father died in 1909, he left the family relatively little money, having lost much of it through bad luck at the racetrack. The family then decided to move to Canada. They booked passage aboard the *Titanic,* but luckily changed their plans at the last minute when the sailing date of the doomed liner's maiden voyage was delayed.

Once on Vancouver Island, Vera, her mother and her brother ran a farm in the Cowichan Valley for two years before moving to Duncan. Eventually Vera bought a house in Oak Bay; her plan was to operate a boarding house in partnership with her sister Kitty, who had by then returned to Canada to be near her family.

Both now single women with no children, Vera and Kitty lavished their affection on their many nieces and nephews. And it was through their favourite niece, Cecily, and her connection to the Matson family, that Vera and Kitty acquired the Rattenbury house on Wollaston Street in 1949.

The two women ran the house as a respectable boarding house for many years, during which time visitors enjoyed the elegant ambience created by the dignity and grace of the sisters. Kitty became ill in the 1970s and eventually died and Vera was left to carry on alone, but the burden of the old house became too much for one elderly lady. When Vera finally died in 1985 at the age of 100, she was laid to rest with her sister in the Cowichan Cemetery in Duncan.

The ashes of one their favourite dogs, Pippi, had been kept in a box in one of Kitty's dresser drawers. The ashes were supposed to have been buried with Kitty when she died, but Vera had forgotten about them; they were eventually buried with Vera.

The sisters' great-nephew, Charles Simmonds, then purchased the home from their estate. It was in need of much repair, and for some years thereafter the house was vacant; its stories from the past remained mysteries, hidden in time.

In the early 1990s, the house magically came to life again when it was bought by Bill and Debrah Patterson, who restored the mansion to its former loveliness. The house received heritage designation in 1994 and is now a seven-unit condominium building that some tenants maintain is haunted.

There is certainly an air of melancholy about this house that visitors have noticed through the years. Archivists who toured the house prior to its renovation in 1993 felt uneasy inside, and sensed a strong atmosphere of gloom surrounding them. Mrs. David Groos, the daughter of R. H. Pooley, who had rented the house at one time, remembered it as being "very sad, dark and dreary." Through time, the house has certainly known some tragedies but the mansion has always held a certain grace and majesty, especially during Vera Easton's reign.

CALEB PIKE HOMESTEAD

The Highlands Sheep Farmer

Young Caleb Pike and his two brothers, William and Jonas, had already led a pretty adventurous life before Caleb settled in the Highlands area of Greater Victoria and built his home there. The three brothers were among 80 immigrants aboard the *Norman Morison* on her first voyage to the Pacific coast. They had left London in October 1849 and sailed around Cape Horn, arriving at Fort Victoria in March 1850.

Caleb, who had just turned 20, was contracted to work for the Hudson's Bay Company for a period of five years at $85 per annum. He worked at the various farms in the immediate area of the fort, among them Craigflower Farm.

It was at Craigflower that Caleb Pike met and became attracted to 16-year-old Elizabeth, the daughter of Duncan Lidgate. Lidgate was an employee of the farm bailiff, Kenneth McKenzie. In those early years of settlement, girls of marriageable age were quickly snapped up, and Lidgate's daughters, Elizabeth and Margaret, were no exceptions. In February 1856, Elizabeth married Caleb Pike; Margaret married William Thompson in December of the same year.

Pike was soon able to buy 40 acres of land in Esquimalt and establish a farm for his bride. The following year their first son, Robert, was born, but he died almost immediately. However, the couple was blessed with seven more children (Helen, Emma, Henry, Charles, Ann, Mary and Elizabeth), a procession that came to a halt when Elizabeth Pike died at 39 in 1878.

For the first years of their marriage, the Pikes resided in Esquimalt at Yew Tree Farm, which was two miles from Esquimalt Harbour and eventually consisted of 286 acres of land, a house, barn, stables and outhouses. The property had an abundant and constant stream of fresh water. They later lived on Wilkinson Road, and still later at a farm between Millstream Road and Thetis Lake, known as Pike Lake Farm. It appears, therefore, that at various times during those early years Pike owned or managed three different farms. Yew Tree Farm was advertised for sale in 1862.

In 1867, Caleb Pike made the headlines. A report in the *Colonist* stated that a certain John Vincent "was charged with punching the head of Caleb Pike and was ordered to find security to keep the peace for three months."

Soon afterwards, Pike moved his family to White Rock on the mainland and their youngest daughter,

~ 1589 Millstream Road ~

named for her mother Elizabeth, was born there just four years before her mother died.

In the late 1870s, Caleb, now a widower in his 40s, returned with his family to the Highlands area, and there in 1878 established his homestead and sheep-and-cattle ranch. His two sons, Henry and Charles, helped him build their home of hand-hewn logs with dovetailed joints. They also built a stable, a roothouse and a woodshed, as well as a large barn and a granary. They produced their own butter, eggs and cream, grew vegetables and raised cattle and sheep. It was an idyllic setting, but farming in the Highlands was a hard life, judging by the small financial returns.

In 1888, Caleb Pike died suddenly, and his obituary in the *Daily Colonist* on January 21rst of that year stated that he had also once owned a farm on the lower Fraser River. He was better known, however, for the establishment of his sheep-and-cattle ranch "among the Goldstream Hills." The obituary closed with the words: "It is seldom that the country is called on to mourn over a pioneer so generally respected as the late Mr. Pike."

The young man of 20 who had come to the colony in 1850 as an illiterate farm labourer (his illiteracy is confirmed by the fact that he signed all documents with an "X") had certainly come a long way and achieved a great deal.

In 1892, Caleb's son, Henry, purchased the homestead along with the 160-acre farm, but soon afterwards he and his brother Charles joined a Victoria sealing fleet and made several trips to the Bering Sea. On one of these dangerous voyages, Henry disappeared while working in a small rowboat alongside a larger vessel, and he was presumed drowned. His family, including his wife back in Victoria, was informed of the sad news, but two years later Henry reappeared on the scene. He had not drowned but had drifted in a rowboat all the way to Japan. It had taken him that long to return to Vancouver Island.

Henry sold the Pike farm and homestead in 1912 and moved to Langford. His brother Charles, who never married, died of cancer in 1924. Henry's sisters had all married and moved away, and his only son, Harold, had died in 1919 following health problems caused by poisonous gas during World War I. When Henry himself died in 1941, therefore, the Pike family name came to an end.

Today, the Highlands area boasts Pike Lake, Caleb Pike Road and Emma Dixon Road (named for Caleb's daughter Emma, who had married Joseph Dixon). But by far the best reminder of this pioneering farming family is the Caleb Pike Homestead at 1589 Millstream Road in Highland Heritage Park. Beautifully restored, it is open to the public for all to enjoy.

THE CONSULATE

A Goldstream Road Mystery

When new owners Bud and Lyn Collins moved into their pagoda-style home at 528 Goldsteam Avenue in 2002, they became intrigued by its history.

The house is a landmark building standing on the corner of Goldsteam Avenue and Van Tilburg Crescent, and many people have long been familiar with it. Some have provided bits of hearsay about its past, the most interesting being the theory that it was once occupied by a Japanese consul and was used as that official's office for a while.

Attempting to unravel the true history of the house proved difficult, and even a visit to the land titles office failed to provide precise information concerning dates. An aura of mystery continues to surround this charming home, which the Collinses have now converted into a delightful bed and breakfast.

While they were renovating the house, the Collinses found a copy of a newspaper clipping stating the house was built for Lavinia Lewis Bailey in 1924 and was to be used as a Chinese art museum. Other records, however, showed that the house was built in 1929 or 1935, that it was designed by architect Hubert Savage, and that proposals for it to be a roadhouse were in the works.

An additional mystery emerged when a gentleman claimed to have worked on building the house during the early 1940s. He clearly remembered the intricacy of the 13 pagodas and the installation of numerous shelves inside the house to accommodate the owners' Oriental artifacts. This may well have been true, and perhaps it was in fact the small adjoining house, built in the same style, which was the one built earlier and then used for storage. That building is no longer there.

Certificates of title, however, place the transfer of the property to the Puget Sound Agricultural Society in November 1921. In 1939 the land was transferred again to one Thomas Shanks McPherson, but there is no indication that present house stood on Lot Number 1 as it now does.

By September 1940, part of the land was under the ownership of Lavinia Bailey, and in 1941 a part was owned by George, Walter, Percy and Archibald Riddle. Subsequent owners were Clifford Ashcroft, Evelyn Mary Jenkins of the quarantine station at William Head, Lavinia Bailey again and in 1955, William Dayton. The following year George and Juliet Noels were listed as joint tenants.

~ 528 Goldstream Road ~

In 1956 Dr. Embert Van Tilburg and his wife Eleanora purchased the property and the pagoda-style house, and they then further subdivided the surrounding lots. Dr. Van Tilburg was something of a pioneer, as doctors were scarce and his practice covered a wide area. He and his wife used their home (and the small adjoining house) to host many Hungarians arriving in Canada after the 1950s revolution in Hungary.

The Van Tilburgs sold the house to the Hallihans in 1964. By 1980 the owners were Roderick and Mary Montagu, who were followed by Kathleen Mottershead, the Lewkes, the Michauds, the Cookes and eventually Bud and Lyn Collins.

This long trail of events and ownership has led the Collinses to believe that their home has been many things during its lifetime. It was definitely a Chinese museum at one time and at another, was a dance studio. It is also known that the house was originally built to take into account the elements of *feng shui,* the 3,000-year-old Chinese practice used to balance the forces between heaven and earth and to ensure that the "sitting and facing" positions of the house are accurate. It is believed that this enables the occupants of the house to remedy existing problems, to enhance wealth and health and to create certain results. Unfortunately, after extensive research, nothing was revealed to substantiate that the house was ever the Japanese consulate.

Nevertheless, a Japanese connection certainly exists. Sometime in the early 1940s, a well-known landscape gardener, Mr. Lahmer, was asked by the owners, Mr. and Mrs. Bailey, to rescue a number of plants, shrubs and trees from the famous Japanese Gardens in Gorge Park, once owned by the Takata family. These included numerous azaleas and rhododendron bushes. The Takatas had been banished from Victoria and sent to detention camps in the interior in April 1942, after the outbreak of war with Japan. Many of these beautiful shrubs still thrive in the grounds of the Pagoda House on Goldsteam.

It would seem that the Japanese consulate connection was just a rumour that somehow got started and then, like Topsy, grew and grew. That has not stopped Bud and Lyn Collins from naming their bed and breakfast "The Consulate," a name sure to perpetuate the delightful aura of mystery of this charming house.

DUNCAN AND THE COWICHAN VALLEY

Heading north from Victoria, the highway known as the Malahat Drive features spectacular views of Saanich Inlet and the Gulf Islands. It has rightfully earned its reputation as one of the most beautiful and scenic roadways in the world. This road was first cut out of steep cliffs and heavy forests as a cattle trail in 1861, although the route had long been used by the Malahat First Nations peoples who had utilized the mountain caves for their spiritual ceremonies.

Malahat Drive climbs over 1,000 feet and Malahat Mountain is considered one of the most sacred sites on the southern portion of the island. In 1884 the road was upgraded to a wagon trail, and by 1911 it had become the first and only paved road to northern Vancouver Island. As the only road north, it soon became an essential highway for settlers who established themselves up-island. The earliest pioneers had travelled north by boat, settling in the Cowichan Valley, Duncan, Nanaimo and beyond.

Driving the Malahat today to visit some of their homes, the explorer comes first to the Cowichan Valley, home of the man who built the town of Mesachie Lake and of an organic farm with an intriguing history dating back to 1894. Also on the list of stops are a 1908 Maclure home designed for an English sea captain; a farmhouse in the Cowichan Valley's Fairbridge community that was once a girls' dormitory in a school; another Maclure mansion on Quamichan Lake; and an inn built on land where a Puget Sound Agricultural Company farmer from Esquimalt resettled his family in 1864.

COULSON HOUSE

The Mesachie Man

Now the prized possession of David and Ulla Coulson, this 1915 house at 5372 Miller Road in Duncan was originally built for Carlton Stone.

Stone was an Englishman born in 1877 who emigrated to Canada, arriving on Vancouver Island in 1910. He built a small steam-powered mill near Fairbridge and developed his own unique method of moving logs; horses pulled empty rail cars up to the logging operation, and when they were loaded, they coasted downhill to the sawmill. By 1917 he had moved his operation to Sahtlam, giving him access to rail transportation (the Esquimalt & Nanaimo Railway) and expanding his market worldwide. That same year Stone's company was incorporated as the Hillcrest Lumber Company and, within 10 years, it was one of the largest companies on Vancouver Island, employing 225 men at the mill and another 100 in the forest.

The lumber ran out eventually and by 1943 Stone was forced to move on. He decided on a site alongside Mesachie Lake. This area, once logged by pioneers, now had a substantial second-growth forest. It also had a legend connected with it concerning a creature, half man, half gorilla, said to have escaped from a sailing vessel wrecked off the west coast. Many locals claimed to have seen or heard this creature, known as the Mesachie Man and believed to live in a cave on Mesachie Mountain.

Stone, however, did not concern himself with legend as he set about building a community beside the lake and in the shade of the mountain. It included a mill, cookhouses, homes for his workers, a church, a playing field and a school; streets were laid out, sewers installed and power provided.

Stone's employees referred to both his company and the village of Mesachie Lake as a family operation. The Stones' son Hector served as president and general manager of the mill, son Gordon was mill manager, Peter was assistant manager, Paul was superintendent of mechanical affairs, and Norman was the mill night manager, so it really was a family business. Stone had also built and financed at least a hundred houses in the Lake Cowichan area itself by the late 1940s, and his mill continued to operate until 1968.

"Stonehaven," the grand estate that Stone built later, is far better known in the area, but the Miller Road house was their first real home, and it was there that Stone and his Welsh-born bride, Ellen Mathias, raised

~ 5372 Miller Road ~

their five sons and one daughter. Stone was very involved in St. Peter's Church in Duncan and gave a generous amount of his money to Queen Margaret's Chapel and St. Christopher's Church in Mesachie Lake. He sold the house on Miller Road in 1926.

The Stones' only daughter, Auriol, married Ted Robertson, the son of a pioneer. Carlton Stone died on October 10, 1950, one day before his 73rd birthday, and Ellen died July 27, 1959.

Later owners of the house on Miller Road, the Bellises, enjoyed entertaining, and the house became well known for its frequent teenagers' parties. When the Coulsons bought the house in 1989, they decided to renovate, but planned to preserve its heritage feel. As a building contractor and heritage-design expert, David Coulson had worked on period homes in Barkerville and the restoration of the nearby town of Wells before he moved to the Cowichan Valley. His wife, Ulla, now owns and runs Ulla's Book Store in Duncan, while Coulson himself is still very much involved in heritage restoration work throughout the island; his interests include the Green Door Fund program in Duncan, which saves derelict heritage buildings, allowing for renovations to be carried out and thereby preventing demolition.

Coulson described his first glimpse of the old Stone house on Miller Road as "breathtaking," for the building seemed to be almost frozen in time. The Virginia creeper clinging to the walls of the house made it look like part of the overall landscape.

The Coulsons have adapted their home to a modern lifestyle while managing to retain the sense of bygone days. For the past 15 years they have worked on converting what they described as "a big, leaky, drafty house with potential" into a home with all the comforts of 21st-century living. The roof has been replaced and the Arts and Crafts style home has been updated with a four-colour paint scheme throughout. Even the Virginia creeper covering the house had a haircut in 2003.

They have also filled the home with antique lamps, furniture and pottery. Terraces, verandas and a conservatory lead into flower and vegetable gardens on the grounds. One greenhouse has windows from the nearby historic Fairbridge Farm school, and a small heritage-style cottage has been added to the property.

David Coulson works in Victoria at least two days a week, knowing at the end of each day he is heading to the haven on Miller Road built for the man who put Mesachie Lake village on the map.

FAIRBURN FARM

An Historic Working Farm with a Loving Ambience

The land surrounding the picturesque Fairburn farmhouse at 3310 Jackson Road in the Cowichan Valley was first homesteaded by Phillip Carvel and John Marriner in 1886. Two years later, John and Mary Jackson bought 40 hectares of that land and built a small temporary homestead which was later moved into Duncan. It was not until 1894 that they built the larger farmhouse on their property on Jackson Road.

John Jackson was born in Ireland and had met his wife, Mary Reid, in Victoria when Mary and her father were visiting from Scotland. The couple married shortly thereafter and it was Mary who decided that the farmhouse they built on their property should be named "Fairburn," meaning "beautiful stream" in the Scottish dialect. The couple had two sons, Edwin and Basil.

The Jacksons raised Jersey cows on their farm and shipped the milk to Victoria. In the early 1900s John Jackson died, but Mary continued the work the couple had begun and was soon raising prize Jersey cows. In 1911, she married a German millionaire, Charles Doering, who had arrived in Canada via the United States in 1885. Doering owned breweries in both Victoria and Vancouver, including the famous Silver Spring Brewery. He also owned the Hat Creek Ranch in the Cariboo which had been established in 1910 after Doering purchased the McCosh, O'Hara and original Hat Creek ranches and amalgamated them. The ranch, located in the Bonaparte Valley near Ashcroft, was a cattle-breeding, horse-breeding and agricultural centre, and Doering also ran the Hotel Hat Creek on the ranch. This eventually became known as the Jackson Ranch when it was later operated by Mary's son Basil Jackson and his wife.

By 1912, Doering had increased Fairburn Farm to 1,200 acres by buying out a number of smaller homesteads. The farm was used as a hunting lodge during the 1920s and there are still caribou and elk heads in the house as reminders of those days of hunting on the island and elsewhere.

Charles Doering passed away in 1927 at age 71, and Mary Doering died in the late 1940s. Her son Edwin, who at that time lived at Mill Bay, put Fairburn Farm on the market. MacMillan Bloedel purchased the mainly forested 1,200 acres for what was believed to be about $1 per acre, but the sale price for the remaining 130-acre farm was slightly higher. The house was then rented out

59

~ 3310 Jackson Road ~

for several years, and by the mid-1950s it had become neglected and rundown.

In 1954, Mollie and Jack Archer purchased the farm as part of the Vancouver Island Organic Produce Co-operative. Participants in the co-operative could buy shares, practise organic farming and receive discounts on supplies. The plan was to use a section of land near the road eventually to build houses for members of the co-operative. The Archers then sold their home in Victoria and lived full-time at Fairburn Farm, which they renamed Kelvin Creek Ranch because part of Kelvin Creek meandered through their property.

Unfortunately, the co-operative soon went under and the farm was almost lost. The Archers spent the next few years paying out the members. The three acres which had been set aside for the co-operative home sites were eventually bought by the Archers' eldest son, Christon.

In order to generate money and at the same time continue to improve the farm, Mollie and Jack Archer and their teenaged son, Darrel, ran a children's camp at the farm during the summer. Mollie also worked full-time as a teacher in the Cowichan Valley, and Jack was an electrician at the Crofton pulp mill. When Darrel left school and Jack retired from the mill, the two men worked full-time on the farm.

Later, Darrel went to Texas to train as a farrier. On his return, he shoed horses to supplement the farm income. Western Riding Stables was then operated from Kelvin Creek Ranch and was available to campers as well as to the general public. This enterprise eventually had to close because of rising insurance rates.

The children's camp continued through the 1960s, with 30 children in three groups of 10, participating in activities such as horse riding, horse husbandry and raku pottery making. At the end of each week, a gymkhana was held by the children who were leaving to welcome the new campers. This event became a highlight for many children who spent happy summers at the ranch.

Mollie Archer was also instrumental in the Family Farm Vacations program, started by the NDP government in the 1970s, which thrived for about 10 years. It eventually folded due to lack of government funding.

In 1978, Mollie and Jack decided to retire, and the farm stopped hosting guests in 1980. In 1982, under the supervision of Darrel and his wife Anthea, the Kelvin Creek Ranch reopened for Family Farm Vacations, but without horses. In 1984, the ranch reverted to its heritage name of Fairburn Farm and in 1993 it became a bed and breakfast.

It had always been the Archer family's dream, however, to make enough money from the farm's operation to ensure its survival without resorting to tourism. While they recognized the educational value of that industry, they longed for some financial stability and hoped the farm would one day be self-sustaining.

For many years they explored the possibilities. Dairy farming had always been of prime interest, but according to the Archers, with the uncertainty of "the cost quota and the quota future with GATT and NAFTA in Canada," investment in that would be unwise. Furthermore, there were so many laws regulating the milk and cheese industries that it made this type of farming more and more difficult.

In October 1998, the Archers read a magazine article on the water buffalo industry in North Devon, England, and they decided to investigate further. Darrel's older brother, Christon, stayed home to take care of the farm, while Darrel and Anthea left for the United Kingdom. After speaking with Bob Palmer, the first person who had processed water buffalo milk into cheese in Lancashire, the Archers were convinced they had found what they had been looking for. They discovered that a herd of water buffalo in Denmark (originally from Bulgaria) was for sale. Denmark and Canada had a reciprocal agreement, as each country was free of the major diseases that these animals could pass on.

In January 2000, 19 Bulgarian Murrah dairy water buffalo, the elite of this species, arrived at Fairburn Farm. One month later the first case of bovine spongiform encephalopathy (BSE) was found in Denmark during a routine slaughterhouse check. That was the only case in 2000, and there were only four more in 2001. Unfortunately, Denmark was now considered a BSE country, so in August 2000 the United States, with Canada following, decreed that all ruminants imported from Denmark during the previous 10 years had to be destroyed.

After a two-year legal battle, the Archers were forced to have all their imported water buffalo destroyed in July 2002. When tested they were all found to be free of BSE and their Canadian-born calves were then freed from quarantine. Unfortunately, all of the Archers' income-producing animals were now gone so the tragedy set them back five years.

By the fall of 2003 they were picking up the pieces and already had their Cowichan Water Buffalo Dairy underway again. A 4,000-square-foot milking parlour was built with a viewing room doubling as an education facility. They anticipate having 15 dairy water buffalo by the fall of 2004, providing enough milk for value-added dairy products. Males over the age of two years will be used for meat. Buffalo meat is 10 per cent lower in fat and 30 per cent lower in cholesterol than beef; because it is pasture raised, the meat is very lean.

So, in spite of their initial setback, the Archers are determined to continue with their goal of making Fairburn Farm the best it can be, with sustainable land that can produce food for future generations. In its pristine setting, the farmhouse is a testament to this determination and love.

THE OLD FARM

A Maclure House Built for a Sea Captain

The simple fact that the house at 2075 Cowichan Bay Road was designed by renowned architect Samuel Maclure makes it of importance. The current owners, George and Barbara MacFarlane, describe it, however, as "spacious and interesting, but it would not be considered one of Maclure's finest when compared with some of the mansions he designed in Victoria."

The house does have an appealing nautical history dating back to the early 20th century, when retired British sea captain William Tooker commissioned Maclure to design a home for him and his family to be built on acreage beside the Cowichan River that he had purchased from Mr. G. T. Corfield. The location, according to *The Cowichan Leader*, held "the finest views in the district for a house to be built." The house itself was described then as "large and commodious, a very fine appearance as would be expected from such a fine architect as Samuel Maclure of Victoria." The house was considered one of the grandest in the district.

Roughly 4,000 square feet in size, it was two storeys high and had an attic that was used as servants' quarters. The house was lit by acetylene lights and heated by hot air circulated throughout by pipes connected to a large hot-water furnace in the basement. The hall and main staircase were finely panelled in rich cedar and the dining room had a beautiful coved ceiling covered with unusual motifs.

The building contractor, W. J. Shearing of Duncan, had the house ready for Captain Tooker, his wife and adult daughters by Christmas 1908. At that time the Island Highway ran directly in front of the house, and apparently the old sea captain liked to drive along it; he was said to be one of the first in the region to own a touring automobile. Undoubtedly the captain was enjoying his retirement years. He had joined the Royal Navy in 1861 as a navigating assistant on the HMS *Victory*, and a large part of his career was devoted to surveying northern and western Australia and, later, Newfoundland.

The Tookers remained in the house until 1919, at which time they moved to the nearby Buena Vista Hotel before leaving for Victoria. Their house was sold to Hugh Beaver, another retired captain, who had served in the Royal Army Medical Corps during World War I. He moved into the house with his wife and daughter. His daughter had served in the land army and then become a

63

~ 2075 Cowichan Bay Road ~

driver in the Women's Royal Air Force (WRAF) during the war. Three years later the Beavers moved on, after holding an auction in the house of all their belongings. The next owner was another short-term one, a Mrs. Fanning.

The Johnstone family, owners during the 1940s and 1950s, were the longest-term residents. During this period a room on the south side was added to the house. The Johnstones were followed by the Killicks, who were the first to operate the house as a bed and breakfast, which they called "Caterham Court." It was later sold to Tony and Karen Davis and Karen's sister, who changed its name to "The Old Farm Bed & Breakfast," in keeping with the Davises' other business, The Old Farm Garden Centre on the highway near Duncan.

In April 1995, the MacFarlanes purchased The Old Farm Bed & Breakfast and have been operating it as such ever since. They have undertaken a great deal of restoration, including the installation of fir floors in the kitchen and downstairs bathrooms. They have attempted to preserve much of the original Maclure flavour and are pleased with the final result.

With all their previous experience in the hotel business, the MacFarlanes have managed to transform The Old Farm the MacFarlanes into a charming place with a delightful country garden that, according to their brochure, is a "collection of evergreen and fruit trees, shrubbery, flowers, berry bushes and vegetable gardens, plus a gazebo."

Here guests can meet, mingle or simply stroll through the grounds, imagining life as it was when the old sea captain lived there.

FAIRBRIDGE FARM

A Social Experiment That Became a Community

Fairbridge Farm on Koksilah Road in Duncan was built in 1935 as part of the Cowichan Valley's Fairbridge Farm community experiment, founded by South African Kingsley Ogilvie Fairbridge.

Fairbridge established the Fairbridge Farm Schools Society in England in 1909. When he first visited England in 1902, he became aware of the incredible poverty and overcrowding in large industrial cities. He was particularly upset by the unhealthy and unstable conditions in which working-class children were forced to live and was determined to do something to improve the situation. In 1909 he returned to England as a Rhodes Scholar, and told fellow students and the Oxford University Colonial Club his plans for saving these children. His idea was to resettle the children in dominions around the world, where they would live together on farms in cottages with "cottage mothers" to take care of them in a village-like setting. The girls would be trained in domestic pursuits and the boys in manual arts and agriculture. It was intended that these young emigrants would then grow up to be productive citizens.

Fairbridge's proposals led to the founding of the Society for the Furtherance of Child Emigration to the Colonies, which afterwards formed part of the Child Emigration Society (CES). The society initially raised £2,000, enabling the first farm school to be set up in western Australia in 1913. Its enormous success inspired others, including the Prince of Wales, to continue to raise funds for more such schools.

In 1935, 11 years after Fairbridge's death, his dream of opening a farm school in Canada finally came true. This new school, officially named the Prince of Wales Fairbridge Farm School, was built on a 1,000-acre property in the Cowichan Valley near Duncan.

The first principal of the facility was Major M. Trew in 1935, followed by Colonel H. T. Logan, 1936–45, Mr. W. J. Garnett, 1945–49 and Major A. H. Plows 1949–51. The site for the farm was named "Pemberlea" because the acreage had formerly belonged to Frederick B. Pemberton, the owner of much prime real estate and many business operations throughout Vancouver Island. In its heyday Pemberlea was a model farm with dairy herds, sheep, poultry and fine horses. Pemberton's milk was shipped daily from Cowichan Station to Victoria, and many prominent Victorians visited the farm. After the stock market crash of 1929, Pemberton lost

~ Koksilah Road ~

practically everything. His last remaining asset was his farm, but he was forced to sell that, too, in 1935.

The house called Fairbridge Farm, now the home of Donald and Colleen MacGregor, was known as the Edith Atwood Cottage when it was a girls' dormitory at the school. Other surrounding buildings form part of the heritage farm school, honouring the memory of a man who had an incredible vision at the turn of the 20th century.

Kingsley Fairbridge died in Perth, Australia, in 1924 at the young age of 39. His health had been weakened due to malaria, which he contracted as a youth. Apart from his life's work for underprivileged children, Fairbridge was a poet of note, and published *Veld Verse and Other Lines* in 1909. His widow, Ruby, a nurse Fairbridge had met at Oxford, praised his works, stating that her husband had had a great understanding of "the native mind and the ways of the animals."

Fairbridge's farm schools prospered around the world and became a monument to him. The one on Vancouver Island continued to operate as a school until 1950, by which time its funding from Britain was running low. Financial problems had first surfaced in 1948 and the Canadian Pacific Railway had offered to lease the estate and bring British farm families to Vancouver Island under the Department of Immigration and Colonization Act. The settlers had to agree to farm the Fairbridge property for at least three years.

Finances prevented the Fairbridge Society from sending any more children or from reopening the estate as a farm school. Finally in March 1950 the school officially closed and the property was rented from the CPR by the B.C. dairy firm Stevenson and McBryde. The dairy took over 70 head of purebred Ayrshire cattle, many tons of grain, farm machinery and household equipment, and a team of Clydesdale horses.

But what of the young Fairbridge Farm graduates? It was said that they certainly repaid their benefactors many times over. Some found food-production jobs and rose in business and professional positions. Many of the girls who had shared the Edith Atwood Cottage became wives and mothers themselves, but still kept in touch with their beloved "cottage mothers" through the Fairbridge Alumni Association. Many still remember Mrs. Brown, the farm manager's wife, who was famous for her delicious cakes.

When Rudyard Kipling died in April 1936, he bequeathed a large part of his estate to the three Fairbridge schools running at that time. This generous gift enabled four more cottages to be built at the Vancouver Island school, and the farm manager was provided with his own house.

Now the cluster of school buildings, including the MacGregors' house, forms a charming village.

The MacGregors moved into their home in 1990 and since then have extensively renovated it to preserve its character. In 1992 the house was reroofed and a detached garage and new deck were added. In 1996 a new kitchen was created. Cabinetry and built-in cupboards appeared there and throughout the house. Dark wood trim was painted white and the walls were painted with brighter colours. What was once the cottage mothers' day room in the schoolgirls' dormitory is now the MacGregors' dining room.

From 1935 to 1950, the Fairbridge experiment proved to be a great success, and today the village and farmhouse continue as a reminder of a piece of fascinating history. Fittingly, the MacGregor home formed part of the Cowichan Valley Heritage House Mother's Day tour in May 2002.

GROVE HALL

The Mansion on the Lake

The magnificent house known as "Grove Hall" overlooking Lake Quamichan on Lakes Road in Duncan started life as a bungalow and eventually grew into a mansion.

This delightful structure was initially designed as a simple bungalow by Samuel Maclure for Captain John Hirsch. Hirsch served in the Boer War with the Strathcona Horse Regiment, a unit which was formed by Lord Strathcona in 1900 as part of the Strathcona Horse (Canadian Regiment). Following that, Hirsch returned to Canada and worked as a land surveyor in Rossland and Nelson. He arrived on Vancouver Island in 1904, and in 1911 he commissioned Maclure to design a bungalow on the old Prevost acreage, which overlooked the lake. Sadly, his wife died soon after and his plans changed.

John Hirsch eventually re-enlisted with his regiment at the beginning of the World War I in 1914 but was wounded and invalided back to Canada in 1915. He died at the age of 68 in 1932, but had long since sold the bungalow at Quamichan to Henry Humphreys, a wealthy importer, who promptly re-commissioned Maclure to design a large extension for the house.

Humphreys was the senior partner in an import-export business that his father had developed in Hong Kong. Born in 1867 in Hong Kong, Humphreys received his education at St. Helen's College in England. In April 1900, he married Eva, and in 1918 they came to the Cowichan Valley and purchased the bungalow from Hirsch, to use primarily as a summer cottage. Humphreys soon developed it into a grand, 22-room home with an Oriental flavour. He also added a 21-by 30-foot billiard room and, being an avid gardener, he transformed the grounds into a spectacular oasis. Twelve Chinese gardeners were brought to Canada by Humphreys to work on the estate, and they lived in the bunkhouse behind the greenhouse. Pathways crisscrossed the acreage and a stone wall was built along the lakefront. He also installed an art-glass skylight in the porte-cochère. According to experts, this is the only Maclure-designed house with such a feature.

The Humphreys called their home "Thorpe" and spent many happy years developing it into one of the most attractive properties in the area. Humphreys was also a keen tennis player and made good use of the tennis court on his property. He always enjoyed the

~ 6159 Lakes Road ~

good life and was a member of the Cowichan Country Club for many years. He still owned horses in Hong Kong and was a member of the yacht and cricket clubs there. From 1915 until 1918, he served with the Hong Kong Defence Corps.

In 1939 the Humphreys sold their large property and moved to Victoria, where they took up residence at the Empress Hotel; Humphreys became a member of the nearby Union Club. He died in August 1944 at age 77.

The next owners of the mansion by the lake were Mr. and Mrs. Frank Ashton who moved there from Vancouver. Frank Ashton was born in Kent, England, and was a well-known member of many horticultural clubs. A chartered accountant by profession, he indulged his hobby of horticulture by continuing to beautify the grounds of the property, which he and his wife renamed Grove Hall. The Ashtons were also prominent in musical circles in Cowichan; he sang and his wife played the piano.

Frank Ashton passed away from a heart ailment in 1943, but his widow stayed on at Grove Hall until 1955. During those years Hugh and Jean Gibson worked at the property — he as gardener and she as housekeeper. In 1968 Gordon and Sheila Johns acquired the property and added the north wing, further enlarging the home.

In 1984 Judy and Frank Oliver purchased Grove Hall as their residence and later turned it into a bed and breakfast. Judy had immediately seen great potential for an incredible home in which she could display the beautiful antiques she had gathered from her world travels. The house and gardens had become somewhat neglected in the years before the Olivers purchased the property; undaunted, Judy restored their luxury.

A Canadian by birth, Judy Oliver earned her nursing degree at the University of Alberta, but her love of travel — especially to unusual and exotic places — took her to work in many parts of the world. Aside from nursing, she also once managed a tourist resort in Fiji and worked for a while at a ski resort in New Zealand.

She travelled through Australia and Indonesia, then on to Singapore, where she nursed in the surgical ward of the Glen Eagle Hospital. It was in Singapore that Judy met her future husband, Frank Oliver, who was an attaché with the American embassy. Later she opened a clinic in Borneo for the staff of Union Oil of California and taught an Indonesian nurse to take over the running of it after she left. Her duties included flying to off-shore rigs and accompanying patients who needed to be flown back to the United States or Singapore.

The initial courtship between Frank and Judy

after they met at the famous Singapore Cricket Club was interrupted by Judy's taking the Borneo job and Frank's return to New York on business, but Frank was persistent and finally persuaded Judy to fly back to Singapore to marry him. He flew in from New York and their wedding took place at the American ambassador's residence in 1974.

Travel was far from over for the Olivers. Their daughter, Alexandra, was born in New York, on September 11, 1975, after which they spent another two years in Singapore and then lived near the Red Sea in Saudi Arabia. While visiting relatives in Victoria at the time her husband was still working as a port manager in Saudi Arabia, Judy came to the Cowichan Valley. Her husband had given her a blank cheque and said "Buy us a place on the water near Victoria" for their anticipated retirement years. But Judy discovered Grove Hall in the Cowichan Valley and promptly fell in love with it. It was, after all, on a lake, even though not too close to Victoria, so she decided on the spot to buy the stately mansion.

The Olivers' belongings arrived at the estate in a convoy of moving vans containing not only their furniture but all the collectibles and antiques that Judy had gathered during decades of travel through China, Indonesia and Saudi Arabia. Grove Hall was the perfect setting for her possessions, and the surrounding grounds (7 acres of garden and a further 10 acres of woodland and fields) merely added to the property's charm. Gradually the Olivers began a restoration program on the house, which has been on-going ever since. By late 1985 they were able to open the mansion as an exclusive bed and breakfast with some of the suites displaying museum-quality antiques and given names such as the "Singapore Room" and the "Indonesian Suite." One of the Olivers' prize possessions is a 400-year-old Chinese wedding bed.

In 2004 Grove Hall and its numerous outbuildings, including the caretaker or guest cottage, a modern five-car garage, an older storage garage for five more vehicles, a six-horse stable, the original bunkhouse for the Chinese gardeners and a greenhouse, was on the market for $2.9 million.

The little Tudor-Revival bungalow of the early 1900s, now with its long private driveway through forest, fenced pasture land and large sweeping lawns and gardens leading down to the lake, has come a long way since those early years. It has evolved into an exquisite mansion with many colourful owners who have loved and cared for it.

It is hoped that future owners will also respect and honour its heritage value.

QUAMICHAN INN

Many Tales from Skinner to Cunningham

The history of the very popular Tudor-Revival-style restaurant on Maple Bay Road and its surrounding land dates back to the 1860s when Thomas Skinner, one of the Puget Sound Agricultural Company farmers, moved his family to the Cowichan Valley from Esquimalt.

The structure itself was not built until 1911. It was a private residence for many years before becoming a restaurant and inn in 1979, to serve as a reminder of the grand social life which was maintained even in the countryside in those early days.

Many decades before the inn was built, however, Thomas Skinner pondered his future at "Oaklands," in Esquimalt. Oaklands had been his home for 11 years since he had arrived with his family from England. He had established a good life in Esquimalt and had prospered, but due to unresolved grievances with the Hudson's Bay Company, he decided it was time to move on to even greener pastures. Nonetheless he still wondered whether he was making a wise decision by uprooting his family and taking them to the "wilderness of the Cowichan Valley" on the 279 acres he had purchased earlier.

The Skinners arrived in the Cowichan Valley in May 1864 aboard the gunboat *Grappler* and settled into a

hard pioneering life, living in tents on their property before a log cabin was built. Eventually they built a larger home, called "Farleigh," which was only the second residence built along the trail later known as Maple Bay Road. Two of the Skinner daughters were married from Farleigh — Annie to John Bremner, a dashing naval officer she had met in Esquimalt, and Constance to a young Victoria lawyer, Alexander Davie, who went on to become premier of British Columbia.

Thomas Skinner died in 1889 at the age of 67 but his widow, Mary, lived on at Farleigh until her own death in 1896, at which time their son Ernest took over ownership of the entire 279 acres. Mary and Thomas Skinner are buried in St. Peter's Cemetery at Quamichan.

In June 1911, Herbert Cunningham Clogstoun purchased 79 acres from Ernest Skinner, who then left the valley and returned to live in Victoria. On this acreage, Clogstoun built the house that is now the Quamichan Inn. Six years later, Ernest and Agnes Paitson purchased the Clogstoun property and called the house Farleigh to honour the memory of the Skinners. In 1921 Ernest Paitson built a large barn on his property to accommodate the prize stock he planned to raise.

~ 1444 Maple Bay Road ~

In May 1924, Eric Springett purchased all the farm buildings and 51 acres from Paitson, and in 1926 C. R. Drayton bought the house, the second Farleigh, from him. Drayton was the manager for Canada and the West Indies of the Union Insurance Society of Canton, whose head office was in Hong Kong. He had been stationed in Toronto and Vancouver, but retired to an advisory position and moved to Cowichan. His wife, Lydia Howland Drayton, was the niece of Sir William Howland, the first lieutenant-governor of Ontario.

That same year Springett built a large log cabin on his part of the acreage for his bride, and during the time the Springetts lived in the log cabin, Mrs. Springett operated a riding school on the property. They also owned and operated the Hiawatha Dairy and Seed Farm there.

In 1935 the Draytons sold their home, now called "Hambow," to Ernest Hall Adams, vice-president of the B.C. Electric Company, and by 1949 the property was registered in the name of Robert Cecil Adams.

A later owner was Marjorie Crane and in 1971 John Harrison was living in the Springett house. He had revitalized the barn as an antique shop, but one week before the scheduled opening, plans changed and the shop was cancelled. In 1979 the Harrisons subdivided the property, but continued to live in the house until 1984.

First to live in the remodelled barn were Leonard and Sally McMahon. Two years later the property was owned by movie producer Tim Zinnemann and his wife, actress Meg Tilly, who stayed until 1989. Other owners included Madeline Chant and Philip Bauslaugh, a college administrator, and Gwyneth Evans, a college instructor.

At the time of the land subdivisions in 1979, the Quamichan Inn, first known as Farleigh and then as Hambow, changed from a private residence into a restaurant when it was purchased by Archie Owen.

Owen was an Englishman who had spent 16 years as a manager of the Odeon theatres in England, plus seven years in the army. He and his wife arrived in Canada in 1957. Owen became manager of the Odeon theatres first in Victoria and then in Duncan; he also managed the Silver Bridge Inn in Duncan. By 1979 the Owens decided they wanted to go into business for themselves so they purchased what is now the Quamichan Inn.

The old Tudor-Revival mansion underwent major renovations and an extension in the hands of the Owens, who wanted to ensure the best food and ambiance for their customers. Soon people came considerable distances to experience the magical atmosphere of the inn.

For the past 20 years the Cunninghams have been the hosts at the Quamichan Inn and have continued to offer the best in dining. The inn by the lake has become a popular place for weddings, banquets or small intimate dinners, nestled in three acres of delightful gardens that once formed part of that large estate pioneered by the Skinner family.

NANAIMO

Incorporated in 1874, Nanaimo is the third-oldest city in British Columbia. Today it is a booming port town with many thriving industries, including forestry, fishing and tourism.

For thousands of years, the sheltered port was inhabited by the Coast Salish people, who called the area *Snuneymuxw*, meaning "The Meeting Place." The present name of Nanaimo is derived from that First Nations word. In the late 1790s, the Spanish explorers Galiano and Valdez discovered Snuneymuxw, but it was another six decades before the settlement expanded, growing up around the Hudson's Bay Company (HBC) fort.

With the discovery of coal, the area began to prosper as a mining centre. In the 1850s there were 10 working mines, and families from England began to settle in what became known as Colvile Town, named for Andrew Colvile, the HBC governor. In 1862 the Vancouver Coal Mining and Land Company bought all the HBC mines.

Scottish-born entrepreneur Robert Dunsmuir became seriously involved in the area's coal business after having apprenticed in the mines for two decades. When the Esquimalt & Nanaimo Railway was completed in 1886, the city's fortunes (and Dunsmuir's) were firmly established. The city of Nanaimo grew and its coal output peaked in 1923, when over one million tons were mined. Nanaimo remained a coal-mining centre until the 1950s.

Houses selected in this section are based on the role they and their residents played in the city's development and evolution. They include a typical miner's cottage, a brick mining office, a rustic mansion built for a wealthy timber baron, a prominent Victorian mansion on what was once the "Nob Hill" of Nanaimo and a residential Victorian cottage typical of many built during the 1890s.

BEBAN HOUSE

A Log-Sided Mansion with a History of Lumber, Horse-Racing and Ghosts

In 1906, Francis Beban emigrated to America from a remote part of New Zealand's Westlands district. He stopped in San Francisco and then, for a while, worked in mining towns in Nevada. In 1907 he headed to Cumberland on Vancouver Island where he contracted to cut pit poles and crossbeams for the Dunsmuir coal mines. In addition, he took a variety of other jobs, including mule-stable foreman for the Extension Mine, south of Nanaimo. An athletic young man, he made quite a name for himself as a first-class competitor in running and wrestling competitions throughout the province.

He quickly realized there was money to be made in the lumber industry, so he purchased a lumber mill at Extension, which was soon reporting a daily output of 50,000 board feet. His fortunes expanded with the purchase of the Empire Lumber Company in 1927 and a coal mine near Extension, which he named the Beban Coal Mine.

By 1930 Beban had become a wealthy lumber baron overseeing a large empire; he also owned a number of racehorses that were housed in one of the largest racing stables in the province. That same year he purchased 160 acres north of Nanaimo. The small farmhouse on the land was soon replaced by a new home for Frank Beban, his wife, Hannah, their three daughters, Evelyn, Dorothy and Verna, and their son, Jack. The house was designed and built by James Green at a cost of $25,000. Over the next 20 years, Frank and Hannah Beban developed this property into a striking country residence featuring exotic gardens and a race track.

The Bebans loved their unique home, which was designed in a rustic style with half-log siding. Steps led up to a large front-entrance porch and a porte cochère covered the side entrance. Although the old-fashioned exterior features lent the appearance of a turn-of-the-century home, the interior was very modern for the 1930s with its five bedrooms, four fireplaces and three tiled bathrooms containing the first coloured bathroom fixtures on Vancouver Island. A large combined living and dining room, a panelled den, some art-deco light fixtures, textured plaster, wainscotting and stained-glass windows are some of the other special features in the home.

~ 2290 Bowen Road ~

Though Frank Beban was well known in business circles he was a very private man. By 1952, his health was not good, but he continued to be an active owner and trainer of thoroughbred horses and tried to keep his spirits up when he was in public. By then his children were married and had moved away so only he, his wife and the servants occupied the large house. On the morning of August 13, 1952, Beban was found dead in his bedroom; he had passed away in his sleep.

The following year, the entire Beban estate was sold to the City of Nanaimo for $53,000 to be used as a sports park, and new outbuildings were added. The rustic old house, however, was sadly neglected and its demolition was being discussed by the early 1990s. Because it was one of the last remaining stately homes in the area and especially because of its unusual architectural style, Nanaimo declared Beban House a heritage site in 1995. With the assistance of the provincial government, the city then began to restore the old mansion.

Since then the house has seen various uses. It has housed a daycare centre, children's summer day camp, RCMP community policing offices, United Way offices and, currently, the headquarters of Tourism Nanaimo.

During the years that Beban House served purposes other than that of private residence, many strange events and weird encounters have occurred, causing even the most skeptical of folk to shake their heads and wonder what's going on in this landmark building.

It all began when some preschool children in the daycare centre started to tell stories about seeing a child playing with a red rubber ball. He was dressed very strangely, they said, in what they thought was a long white nightgown, and his black hair was tightly braided. The administrators asked the children to draw what they assumed was an imaginary playmate and were amazed to find that they had all drawn a similar picture. Researchers later discovered that a young Chinese boy, the son of one of the Bebans' servants, had died in the house. It had been assumed the children were drawing a small girl, but the long braid could have been the traditional pigtail worn by Chinese men. Even the general manager of Tourism Nanaimo frequently heard footsteps similar to those of a child running up and down the stairs. This little lost spirit seemed to appear only to other children though — they were the ones who actually saw the child.

Other strange happenings have also occurred. A cupboard door in what was once Frank Beban's trophy room kept opening on its own and refused to close. A filing cabinet drawer in one of the offices also kept opening for no apparent reason. Creaks and groans have often been heard on the staircase. The tinkling of teacups and the sound of women's voices can often be heard coming from an unoccupied room. A loud yell disturbed the quiet on one occasion. Another time, stomping occurred on the floor of the upstairs bedroom in which Frank Beban died. Lights burn in the house at night when it is empty. Worse, a boiler room once used by the Chinese servants as living quarters is now a cold, bleak area with an eerie atmosphere. A psychic was once invited to go down to investigate, but found it so unpleasant that she could hardly breathe. She refused to go there again.

For the past few years at the beginning of each summer season, the staff have arrived to find that all the doorknobs in Beban House have been unscrewed. Weird, unintelligible messages have been left on voice mail at night, and dust once suddenly fell from the ceiling in one office, again for no obvious reason.

Thumps, creaks, bangs, a running toilet upstairs and even flying objects could perhaps all be explained, but many happenings are totally mystifying. For instance, an RCMP officer claimed to have seen a woman standing outside the United Way's office when there was no one there. On another occasion, an employee clearly witnessed a woman standing in the doorway of her office dressed in a long blue gown. The employee walked toward the woman to ask if she could help her, thinking she had entered the building through the back door by mistake. The woman went around the corner toward the lobby and then literally disappeared into thin air. No one was there.

These many apparitions seem to be more prevalent at Halloween and Christmas. One might wonder why there is so much energy from spirits in the house, but the staff seem unperturbed by the many ghosts, which appear to be harmless, though somewhat irritating on occasion.

The unique home Frank Beban created and enjoyed with his family so long ago continues to function in many useful ways, as well as being full of intrigue with its ghostly stories. It remains a landmark presence on Bowen Road.

A MINER'S COTTAGE

Reminder of Another Era

This modest little house, which now sits in Piper's Park adjacent to the Nanaimo District Museum, was moved from its original location at 830 Farquhar Street in the 1970s. Today a designated municipal heritage site, it serves as a reminder of the kind of accommodation in which mineworkers and labourers in Nanaimo once lived.

In 1872 Yorkshireman Frederick Rowbottom arrived in Nanaimo and by 1887 he was able to purchase some land. By 1890 he was working for the Vancouver Coal Mining and Land Company (VCMLC), and it's believed he built this particular little house for his family about 1897.

Coal was discovered on Vancouver Island in 1835 at Fort Rupert, and the Hudson's Bay Company (HBC) mined there for several years, eventually abandoning the site; mining did not start in the Nanaimo area until 1851. By 1862 the HBC decided to sell its coal mines, machinery, buildings, sawmill, wharves and land — including Newcastle and Douglas (now Protection) islands — to the VCMLC. That company continued operating successfully, increasing its coal output each year until the 1890s. About 1,500 men, including Rowbottom, were employed in these mines, which had names such as Old Douglas Shaft, New Douglas and Chase River Mine and Fitzwilliam Mine. There was very little competition for the VCMLC until 1871, when Robert Dunsmuir began developing the Wellington Mines north of Nanaimo.

Rowbottom did not work long for the VCMLC. He moved on to his other trade of stone masonry and was responsible for the stonework on the old Nanaimo Opera House and the Queen's Hotel. He died in 1909 at the age of 60 and his wife Mary Ann lived on in the four-room house until 1917, at which time she sold it to Emma Eliza Kemp. Soon after that sale, another house and Manson's General Store were built alongside the Rowbottom cottage. In 1941 Jane Agnes Beck acquired the property from Kemp, and she passed it on to her son 11 years later.

In 1955 the house again had new owners, the Arthur Sutton family, who in 1977 donated the cottage to the Nanaimo Historical Society when a road-widening project at Farquhar would have meant its demolition. It was moved to Piper's Park on Cameron Road and given municipal heritage designation in 1980.

~ 100 Cameron Road ~

Few of the early miners' cottages remain today in their original format and shape. Most were either enlarged to accommodate growing families or demolished. Some, like this one on Cameron Road, moved. A few others can still be found on Haliburton Road in the older part of Nanaimo. Although the history of this particular cottage and its inhabitants is sparse, it clearly portrays an excellent example of the modest housing that Nanaimo's early miners and labourers called home.

McKECHNIE HOUSE

Victorian Residence on "Nob Hill"

This late-Victorian house towering above the others at 546 Prideaux Street has been a prominent landmark since the 1890s. It is situated in an area once known as the "Nob Hill" of Nanaimo.

It was said to have been built around 1894 for the Honourable Dr. Robert E. McKechnie, the medical doctor for the Vancouver Coal Mining and Land Company. Evidence also exists that suggests it might have been built slightly earlier and lived in briefly by Judge Eli Harrison and his wife, Eunice, before they took over the Dunsmuir residence near Departure Bay. In any event the house was one of the largest of its kind in Nanaimo. It sported intricate roof lines and a central front entry leading to a double-height stairwell. The staircase itself still retains its fir panelling, balustrades and newel posts, but the interior has been divided into suites and the original siding has been stuccoed.

Dr. McKechnie was born in Brockville, Ontario, in 1861, and began his studies at McGill University in 1886. He did his internship at the Montreal General Hospital and moved to Nanaimo in 1891, where he practised medicine for the next 10 years. He was elected to the Council of the College of Physicians and Surgeons of British Columbia in 1896 and served as its president in 1897, 1906 and 1910.

In 1898 he was elected as member of the legislative assembly for Nanaimo and served as minister without portfolio in the government of Premier Charles Semlin. In 1899 he was elected the first president of the B.C. Medical Association. The house on Prideaux Street was a suitable setting for Dr. McKechnie but, after spending some time in Europe, he decided to move his practice to Vancouver, where he lived for the remainder of his career. He died in Vancouver in 1944.

After the McKechnies left the house on Prideaux, it was purchased by Dr. James H. Hogle who used it to accommodate his female patients, since the hospital in Nanaimo did not provide beds for women at that time. Dr. Hogle was also one of the first owners of an automobile in the city, having purchased his in March 1907.

Between World Wars I and II, the house was transformed into a boys' residential and day school modelled on the English boarding-school system. Most of the boys who attended St. George's-On-The-Hill had parents who were travelling or lived abroad. The school

~ 546 Prideaux Street ~

gained a reputation among those who attended it as an alternative to jail, so it obviously had stringent rules.

Just before World War II, a Texas man named Shelby Saunders bought the house and divided it into suites for the wives of soldiers serving abroad. Saunders also owned and ran the Pygmy Pavilion on Chapel Street, a dance hall that became very popular with soldiers stationed in Nanaimo during the war.

Once the home of a doctor, a politician and a judge, this grand old house on Nob Hill continues to dominate the area in its current capacity as an apartment building.

THE MINING OFFICE

A Brick Cottage on Jingle Pot Road

Around 1910 a small brick building, now located at 1904 Jingle Pot Road, was constructed as an office for the local Jingle Pot Mining Company. On its original site it also had a rear addition that included a concrete milk house.

By the 1920s the little office building had been converted into a house and was occupied by the Specogna family. The original portion of the converted house had an offset front entry and segmented arched windows and door openings. Its address then was 1881 Jingle Pot Road. The house originally stood on a large corner lot off Addison Road and the surrounding acreage was farmland. Many agricultural buildings also surrounded the little brick house.

According to Nanaimo archival records, "This small brick house is a highly unusual variation of early miners' housing — it is the only such early brick house known to have survived." Even though nearby East Wellington was a brick-and-tile manufacturing area, brick was apparently seldom used for residential work.

In 1999, the house was relocated on Jingle Pot Road to accommodate proposed road construction, and ownership was transferred to the City of Nanaimo. The brick building is currently used as an environmental and historical interpretation centre for the adjoining Buttertubs Marsh and Harewood neighbourhood.

Buttertubs Marsh is man-made wetland, and was officially opened in 1977. One of only a few marshes in British Columbia found inside city limits, this wildlife sanctuary came about because of the hard work of Nanaimo field naturalists, local and provincial governments and private organizations.

Poplars and oaks line the borders of the marsh as reminders of the history of this land when it was wooded and formed part of a farm owned by the Western Fuel Company. The rather odd name of "Buttertubs" was not used until the mid-1970s when the owner of the property proposed a housing development on his land and decided to name it Buttertubs after an area in Yorkshire, England. Though the housing proposal was not passed by the ministry of environment, the name Buttertubs remained.

The original "buttertubs" are a series of deep limestone holes, many of which, according to local folklore, are "bottomless" and some "even deeper than that!" It was said that the monks who lived in the area long ago

~ 1904 Jingle Pot Road ~

stored their cheese and butter in these deep holes, hence the name. Buttertubs Pass lies between Wensleydale and Swaledale in the North Yorkshire Dales.

The Nanaimo Field Naturalists have been heavily involved with this wildlife sanctuary since the 1970s, as have the City of Nanaimo, Ducks Unlimited, The Nature Trust of British Columbia and The Land Conservancy, all of whom have worked to allow this incredible haven to exist a mere two kilometres west of Nanaimo. Waxwings, great blue herons, Canada geese, American widgeon, red-winged blackbirds and green swallows are just a few of the birds to be seen there, and Buttertubs is believed to be the only breeding site of American bitterns on Vancouver Island.

It is particularly rewarding to note the rather paradoxical evolution of this little brick house, so symbolic of Nanaimo's coal-mining past, from mining-company office to family residence and then to an interpretive centre for a tranquil wildlife sanctuary. Past and present have been united in a unique and rewarding way.

GILBERT HOUSE

A Victorian Cottage with an Eclectic Past

Soon after their arrival in Canada from Cornwall, England, John Gilbert and his wife, Mary Jane, opened The Temperance House in Nanaimo, a boarding house at the corner of Bastion and Skinner streets. Board was $6 per month, and by all accounts, the Gilberts did well and made a good living.

Following the death of John Gilbert in 1876 and his brother William in an 1887 mine explosion, Mrs. Gilbert had this delightful Victorian cottage built for herself at 279 Selby Street in 1893 and lived in it until her own death in 1898 at the age of 60. When her house was being built, she also reopened The Temperance House as a means of generating income.

Although the Gilbert house still sits on its original site on Selby Street, it has been changed considerably over the years from its original Italianate style with two storeys. Square and symmetrical in design with a central front entry, it has front bay windows that feature the original decorative carved brackets at the eave line.

Following Mrs. Gilbert's death, her son, John, who had been a trader on the Nass River and then a machinist, continued to live in the house for a few years. Eventually he moved to Vancouver, where he died in 1926.

Mrs. Gilbert's daughter, Laura, married George Cavalsky in 1887. She was given away by John Pawson, a former mayor of Nanaimo. George Cavalsky owned a store on Bastion Street and he and Laura were a prominent part of pioneer society life in Nanaimo. Their store became the site of the first telephone exchange in Nanaimo. The very first telephone system in British Columbia ran from the Dunsmuir Mine at Wellington to the dock at Departure Bay, but once the Nanaimo Telephone Company was incorporated in 1890 and took up operations in the Cavalsky Store, Laura Cavalsky became the first telephone operator.

Meanwhile, the Gilbert family home on Selby Street was acquired by A. E. Mainwaring. In the 1950s, a fire at the house gutted the top storey, which was then removed. The house now has a pyramidal roof that extends over the two front bays, forming a smaller roof to cover the porch.

The front garden still has numerous mature shrubs and landscape features typical of its period, including variegated holly bushes.

Today the house accommodates law offices, but it has retained one of its most remarkable features. Still

~ 279 Selby Street ~

standing are the unique wrought-iron front gate and gateposts, which were manufactured by the Stewart Iron Works Company, then of Cincinnati, Ohio, but now located in Kentucky. It is unusual today to find any wrought-iron on older houses in this area because during World War II most cast metal was removed in the many patriotic scrap-metal drives.

PORT ALBERNI

Heading west toward the Pacific Rim region of Vancouver Island, we find Port Alberni at the head of Alberni Inlet, a narrow fjord that almost bisects the island. In 1860 nine men landed at the head of this inlet to establish a sawmill on land that was occupied by First Nations peoples. Two communities developed: Alberni, where the settlers lived, and Port Alberni, the site of the docks from which lumber was shipped. The name was chosen to honour Don Pedro Alberni, an army captain with the Spanish troops garrisoned in the area in 1791.

By 1866 the nearby trees had all been cut down, so the sawmill machinery was removed. A paper mill was then established but it only operated for a few years. Most pioneer settlers left the valley, but the arrival of the Esquimalt & Nanaimo Railway in 1911 gave Port Alberni a second lease on life. The heavily forested areas farther out were soon being logged, mills were beginning to operate and a plywood plant and pulp and paper mill were in production. Big money was being made.

An earthquake in Alaska in 1964 caused a tsunami, or tidal wave, to sweep up Alberni Inlet, destroying much of the lower regions of the two cities. In 1967 the twin cities were amalgamated, making Port Alberni the fifth-largest city in British Columbia.

Tourism is a big industry in the valley today, and Port Alberni vies with Campbell River as the Salmon Fishing Capital of the World. One of the biggest tourist attractions lies east of Port Alberni at Cathedral Grove on Highway 4. There, Douglas fir, western hemlock and western red cedar, some over 800 years old, tower skyward to 200 feet (62 metres).

Three houses in Port Alberni have been selected for this section: a Maclure-designed home built for Captain Hodgson, the land surveyor who planned the townsite of Port Alberni; the house on the hill where Thomas Paterson and his heroine wife, Minnie, once lived; and the Clark house that sits high above the town on 7th Avenue and has intriguing tales, both sad and happy, of past residents.

KITSUKSIS

A Maclure House in the Wilderness

Captain M. H. T. Hodgson, an Englishman educated at Harrow and University College in London, became a civil engineer and then emigrated to Canada. Before that he had spent time as a trooper in the Boer War. In 1905 he worked for James Dunsmuir on the survey for the Esquimalt & Nanaimo Railway, and grew to love Vancouver Island's wilderness with a passion.

Soon after his arrival in Canada, Captain Hodgson met and married Eleanor Butler, a nurse from Lincolnshire, England. She was a woman far ahead of her time with an adventurous and free-thinking spirit that brought her to Victoria, where she fell in love with the captain. Hodgson took his bride to Alberni by stagecoach in 1908 and their first home was a log house at the end of Margaret Street, which was then called Creamery Road. By 1913 he had completed his B. C. Land Surveyor qualifications and opened up his own office in Alberni. His later jobs included the laying out of the Port Alberni townsite and the triangulation survey of the west coast of the island between Barkley Sound and Ahousat.

Hodgson's work took him all over the island, keeping him very busy and leaving little time for hobbies. In 1913, he commissioned Samuel Maclure to design a house for his family high above Kitsuksis Creek. The house would overlook the valley and be surrounded by 15 acres of forest. It was not designed to be a pretentious or flamboyant home; it was simply a family home that would accommodate the needs of the Hodgsons' growing family.

It soon became a happy place for their four children (three daughters and a son) to grow up in, with its two storeys, large kitchen, study, playroom and five bedrooms. Both the drawing room and the dining room were finished in cedar panelling and a long veranda fronted the length of the house. The veranda was especially pleasant on humid summer nights in the Alberni Valley.

The Hodgsons were very active in their community. They were both staunch members of All Saints Church, where the captain served as lay reader for more than 40 years. They were also members of the Alberni Tennis Club, and Mrs. Hodgson did a great deal of work for the Red Cross, holding Red Cross parties and church bazaars in the garden at Kitsuksis during World War I. Captain Hodgson was by then serving in France with the Royal Engineers.

— Kitsuksis, Port Alberni —

Eleanor Hodgson was the first woman in Port Alberni to drive a motor car, and during the 1918 influenza epidemic she used her skills at the Indian Residential School as a volunteer nurse. She also briefly served as an alderwoman and was northern Vancouver Island's first Girl Guide Commissioner. She founded and worked tirelessly for the Alberni Junior Hospital Auxiliary. Her love of flowers and involvement in horticultural societies helped produce a delightful garden at Kitsuksis, which became a showplace through the years.

Mrs. Hodgson also loved her home. With the assistance of a governess to help with the children's education until they were old enough for boarding school, and a Chinese man who worked both in the house and in the garden, she was able to run her home with care, furnishing it to harmonize with its natural setting.

The Hodgsons and their four children all left their mark on the community. Their son and one daughter became teachers; the two other daughters followed their mother into nursing.

As a couple, the Hodgsons were ideally suited to each other. He was the epitome of the English gentleman — he enjoyed the outdoors, his cocker spaniels always by his side, or he could be found reading one of his numerous books, playing his piano for relaxation and writing many pieces of music himself. His wife provided a happy, peaceful home.

Surprisingly, Kitsuksis has only had three owners during its 91-year history. The year after Captain Hodgson's death at the house in 1958, the family sold it to local residents George and Amy Dent. The Dents then modernized the house extensively, but retained the feel of the old family home. It was designed and built with family living in mind and that was how it remained — only the use of certain rooms was altered. For example, a second-floor master bedroom once occupied by Mrs. Hodgson's mother, who frequently visited from England, was converted into a dance studio for the Dents' daughter, Sharon, a well-known instructor in the valley. Sharon's own bedroom in the house was once the Hodgson children's schoolroom. Captain Hodgson's ground-floor study became the place where Sharon and her brother, Jim, did their homework.

The Dent family did much to upgrade and redecorate the home during their almost 20-year residence, and were sad to sell the house in 1979. It still needed more work but further renovations meant more money, so they were unable to continue.

The current owners then took up the challenge and have continued the tradition of family living. Although they have renovated and updated through the years, they have kept the integral heart of the house intact. They modernized the kitchen, reroofed the house, and rebuilt portions of the veranda. In addition, old deadbolt locks from the St. Francis Hotel in San Francisco have been installed throughout.

Today Kitsuksis sits at the end of a long and winding road in Port Alberni, on a plateau overlooking the creek for which it was named. Mrs. Hodgson, the first lady of the house, once said that "many visitors had stayed at Kitsuksis from all parts of the world, but there was also always room available for anyone in need, a place where the weary could find rest and refreshment."

The captain, who loved the outdoors and the Alberni Valley, would have thought her comment a fitting memorial to the house he built with love.

PATERSON HOUSE

Where a Heroine Lived

It was once merely dubbed "the house on the hill" and today, long after it was built in 1907, this large, white, majestic house still sits proudly high up on Paterson Place overlooking the Alberni Valley. Now it is better known simply as the old Paterson House.

Through the years this house has had many owners, but its importance as a heritage building is due mainly to its first owner, who actually only lived there for three years. The fame of that first resident, Minnie (Huff) Paterson, dates back to a stormy night in December 1906.

At that time Minnie was the wife of Thomas Paterson, the Cape Beale lighthouse keeper. Her heroic actions on the night in question gained attention around the world and are the reason why the Paterson House is still thought of today as a memorial to this gallant lady, described by many as "the Grace Darling of the west coast."

Grace Darling was a heroine in Victorian England who bravely rowed out from the lighthouse where her father was the keeper to save nine survivors clinging to rocks after the SS *Forfarshire* ran aground on the Farne Islands in September 1838. Grace was just 23 years old and was considered to be "pious and pure, modest and yet so brave," a description that might easily have been applied to Minnie Paterson as well. Grace's ordeal that night shortened her young life; she died three years later of tuberculosis and is buried at Bamburgh Church in England.

It seems that Minnie Paterson also led an adventurous life. As a small girl growing up in the Alberni Valley, Minnie had to cross the Somass River every day in a rowboat in all kinds of weather to attend the Alberni School. She was one of the school's first pupils. She also walked on trails where cougars roamed, and lived with her family in a log cabin in the wilderness. Pioneer times were rough for settlers and, for this reason, Minnie was no stranger to courage.

She grew up and married Scotsman Tom Paterson, who had worked in Seattle before arriving in the Alberni Valley, and she and their first child willingly accompanied Tom to the Cape Beale lighthouse two years after their wedding, when Tom was offered the job of lighthouse keeper.

Minnie's work alongside her husband was invaluable as she assisted in guiding ships to safety on many occasions. The passenger ship *Valencia,* which lost course

~ 4660 Paterson Place ~

in a dense fog, provided just one example of Minnie's dedication to her fellow man. She cared for many of the survivors before they were transferred to hospital, and worked tirelessly to save lives — this just three weeks before her second child, a son, was born. The Patersons eventually had five children in all.

But it was the night of December 6, 1906, that made Minnie Paterson famous around the world and earned her many accolades. As a fierce storm raged around them, Tom called Minnie to tell her that he had spotted the barque *Coloma* in distress off Cape Beale. The *Coloma* had left Port Townsend carrying lumber bound for Australia, but had been caught in the storm, which blew out her sails and masts. She was now dangerously near the rocks and had her flag flying upside down, signalling distress. Tom could see the nine-man crew and Captain Allison desperately clinging to the stump of the mast, but knew there was only one way to save them. He had to make contact with the lighthouse tender *Quadra,* which was sheltering from the horrendous storm at Bamfield, some six miles away. Unfortunately all telephone communication had been broken off by the storm. Tom himself could not leave the light and the foghorn, so without another thought Minnie told her husband that she would make the trip over rocks

and through the woods. Although Tom was reluctant to allow his young wife to undertake this perilous journey in the dark, he had no choice. They knew that the responsibilities of lighthouse keepers meant being able to deal with emergencies such as this one.

Accompanied by their family dog, a collie named Yarrow, Minnie immediately set off on foot over the dangerous terrain. She waded waist-deep across Bamfield Creek, cut through more deep bush and eventually arrived at the home of linesman James McKay, only to be told by Mrs. McKay that her husband was away trying to repair breaks in the line. Minnie and Mrs. McKay then pushed a small boat out themselves and rowed through the high waves to where the *Quadra* lay anchored. Minnie delivered her message to the captain and the *Quadra* raced under full steam to the *Coloma* to rescue her captain and crew. Mere minutes afterward, the *Coloma* went down and broke into pieces on the rocks.

Meanwhile, the two women rowed back to shore. Although Minnie was soaked and badly scratched from falling on rocks into icy-cold water and trudging knee-deep in mud, she refused Mrs. McKay's kind offer of rest and new clothing. She insisted on returning at once the same way she had come, saying that she had to get back because her baby needed her. With Yarrow once more at her heels, she set off on the trail back to Cape Beale. One week later, when the telegraph line was finally repaired, she learned that the captain and crew of the *Coloma* had all been saved.

Praise began to come in from many quarters once news of Minnie's heroism spread. Letters of congratulations arrived from Ottawa and from the American Consular Service. She was presented with a silver plate by the Dominion government, acknowledging her bravery, as well as a silver tea service "presented for Valour."

Citations praising this brave woman were numerous, but perhaps the one her family valued the most came from the Sailor's Union of the Pacific:

Whereas, Mrs. Thomas Paterson of Cape Beale, Vancouver Island, has repeatedly, at the risk of her health and life, proven herself a heroine by assisting in saving the lives of unfortunate castaways on the rocky shores of her chosen home, or adrift in the nearby ocean, therefore, be it, by the Seattle Branch of the Sailor's Union of the Pacific in meeting assembled RESOLVED that we, the Seamen of America

fully recognize her sterling worth as the highest type of womanhood, deeply appreciating her unselfish sacrifices in behalf of those "who go down to the sea in ships" and assure her and hers of our undying gratitude.

In 1907 Tom Paterson left the life of the lighthouse keeper and built a family home in Port Alberni for his wife and children, but sadly, Minnie was only able to enjoy her big house for four years. She died in 1911 from pneumonia, never having fully recovered from the strain and long exposure to the elements on that December night.

The Paterson house in Port Alberni changed hands a few times after the family sold it. A 1979 real-estate advertisement described it as "a unique home containing seven bedrooms, large formal dining room, living room with an unusual fireplace, and a full basement." The owner had considerably modernized the house by then and yet retained a feeling of the past. Situated on a half-acre lot with "magnificent views of the Valley," it was priced at $53,500 at that time.

Its heritage, however, is priceless.

CLARK HOUSE

Ill-Fated Love and a Peaceful Resting Place

According to records, the house at 2950 7th Avenue in Port Alberni was the first to be built on the hill once referred to as "Nob Hill," a name given because only the wealthy could afford property there.

That whole area was known as New Alberni to distinguish it from the old town (Alberni), which was built up around Johnson Street. In 1910 New Alberni became Port Alberni and was incorporated as such in 1912. The land on the hill originally belonged to the Anderson Company from England, which then formed the Alberni Land Company. They in turn surveyed and subdivided the area into lots.

In 1905 a Mr. Clark built a small house on Lots 3 and 4. That house, now much larger, is the subject of this story. Around 1910 two more houses were built on Lots 6 and 7, one for James Beatty Wood and the other for his brother, A. Beatty Wood. James became the first fisheries officer for Alberni, serving from 1912 to 1937.

In 1921 John Owen Halliwell Walcot of Cowichan Station purchased Lots 3 and 4 and the buildings on them, but the following year the owner of the property was Elmer S. Glaspie, the superintendent of the Alberni Pacific Lumber Company. Glaspie altered the small house by adding four wings, two on either side of the large veranda overlooking the Alberni Canal on the west side, and two on the east side. He and his mother lived in the house for many years and, during that time, he became friends with Mary Wood, the daughter of neighbour James Wood. The couple had what was, in those days, considered "an understanding."

Mary Wood lived in her father's house for most of her life and during the 1920s and early 1930s considered Elmer her unofficial beau. Elmer, however, obviously thought otherwise and, much to everyone's surprise, in December 1933 he took Poppy Vivienne Beale as his bride in a ceremony at the Bishop's Palace in Victoria, followed by a reception at the Empress Hotel. The bride was stunning in a gown of white suede velvet and carried a shower bouquet of deep red roses and lily-of-the-valley. After a honeymoon in the United States, the couple returned to the house on the hill.

Mary's dreams of becoming Mrs. Glaspie were dashed. The end of what she considered their romance may have occurred due to a difference in religious beliefs, or simply because Elmer had never felt committed to Mary. Whatever the reason, Mary Wood stayed single for the rest of her life.

~ 2950 7th Avenue ~

Eventually the Glaspies moved to Vancouver. Another owner of the house was Martha Ida Clarke, but in 1938 the house was purchased by Allen H. Wylie, the manager of the Bank of Montreal. Wylie was also a founding member and first treasurer of the Rotary Club, and a member of the Bivouac Club of Port Alberni. The house was purchased in 1949 by Dr. William Laurence Chisholm and his wife Ruby, who spent many happy years there with their children, Leslie and Duncan. Dr. Chisholm retired in 1968 and the house changed hands again. The new owners, David and Ellen Davis, lived in the house for three years.

In 1971 the house was purchased by Richard and Marta Williamson. Their son, Travers Bout Williamson, was the first child actually born *in* the house. The Williamsons renovated quite extensively during the 1970s, turning the middle part of the porch into a dining room, removing the French doors between two back bedrooms and adding an ensuite bathroom. They also gutted and rebuilt the main bathroom in 1978 and added a double garage to the house in 1986. The original living room, built in 1905, has never been changed. It still features dark, high wainscotting, and its floor is also original. The den and entrance hall, once the dining room, are also unchanged from the late-1920 renovations by Elmer Glaspie. The pine wainscotting in the entrance hall is original, but the oak floor is new.

Elmer Glaspie created a large garden, planting cedars, pink dogwoods, weeping cherry trees, holly trees, viburnum, mock orange trees and yew trees. He also dug a large pond, and planted three poplar trees on the west side, which were removed in 2002 due to age. To help him in those early days, Glaspie hired a Japanese gardener.

In 1972 Richard Williamson and his father planted a cedar hedge and ivy, which came from the Williamson family's lakeside home and had been grown there by Richard's grandfather, after whom Williamson Park is named.

In 1999 Marta Williamson started to garden again in earnest, blending the new with the old. Today the house is still owned and lived in by Marta, who treasures and guards its history. During her many conversations through the years with Mary Wood, who passed away in 1996 at the age of 92, she learned the story of Mary's attachment to Elmer Glaspie. Mary gave Marta Williamson many photographs of those early days, including a formal picture of Mr. Glaspie himself.

Also during Mrs. Williamson's residency in the house on the hill, she was visited one day by Dr. Chisholm's daughter, Leslie, who had come with an unusual request. Her parents had now both passed away and she asked if their ashes might be placed in the garden of 2950 7th Avenue.

The elegant home on the hill overlooking the Alberni Valley obviously held many happy memories.

PARKSVILLE AND QUALICUM BEACH

Heading northwest, our next stops are Parksville and Qualicum Beach, the two holiday hot spots on Vancouver Island.

It wasn't always that way, though. Before 1910, Parksville was known simply as The River, a quiet, virtually unknown village with few residents. Once the Esquimalt & Nanaimo Railway made a stop there, the name was changed to McBride Junction. Soon after that, the name was changed again to Parksville to honour Nelson Parks, the first postmaster in 1886. Parks's cabin once stood where the community park is located today.

Qualicum Beach had its beginnings around 1911 when a financial syndicate known as the Merchants Trust and Trading Company purchased land in the area and set about subdividing it for tourism purposes. A golf course and a hotel, the Qualicum Beach Inn, were built around that time. The name Qualicum comes from the First Nations word *Qualwho*, meaning dog (chum) salmon, which are plentiful in the two rivers north of Qualicum.

The houses from these two areas cover a wide spectrum. We begin with a Maclure house that is now a well-known inn and restaurant in Parksville. Also included are a Sears-Roebuck house in Qualicum Woods, which was shipped from Chicago by train and boat; an elegant home and estate where royalty have been entertained; Qualicum's first designated heritage house, initially built as a summer home; a large white house that dates to 1912 and is now occupied by a hospice; and a mansion once owned by General Noel Money, one of Qualicum's pioneers.

Many more stories lie behind these varied walls.

Newbie Lodge

From Elegant Residence
to Popular Inn and Restaurant

Nestled among acres of woodland, the Maclure-designed house once known as "Newbie Lodge" is both charming and unique.

It was built in 1921 at an estimated cost of $50,000 (a veritable fortune at that time) for wealthy businessman Matthew P. Beattie, a native of Scotland who had lived in Hong Kong prior to coming to Victoria. Samuel Maclure designed the house for Beattie and his bride, nurse Evelyn Gibbs, the daughter of Samuel Gibbs, a landowner in Parksville. Matthew and Evelyn had met in Victoria when he was one of her patients in hospital and they had instantly fallen in love. After they were married, Beattie purchased 40 acres of land from his father-in-law to build a dream home about one mile south of Parksville.

At that time Parksville was still somewhat isolated. The road from Nanaimo had only been extended to Parksville in 1886, and another 10 years passed before this road was connected to Qualicum, a distance of only 10 miles. At the turn of the century the road finally reached Comox and by 1904 it went as far as Campbell River. However, during the 1920s when Newbie Lodge was built, roads were often unreliable and treacherous; sometimes they were unpaved or surfaced with graded gravel, but most often they were simply dirt tracks with large potholes. In the early days, the 40 miles between Nanaimo and Parksville took six hours to travel with team and buggy, and it took a day and a half by stagecoach to get from Nanaimo to Alberni.

Although communication had improved greatly with the coming of the Esquimalt & Nanaimo Railway, Parksville was still considered wilderness in the 1920s and any excursion there would have been thought of as a "country jaunt" or a daring adventure.

The Beatties' new home, Newbie Lodge, was named after Newbie House in Annan, Scotland, and was designed in the style of a hunting lodge. Maclure's experiments with the chalet-style design and cross-axial plan are apparent. Maclure always insisted on superior tradesmen working on his design from paper to reality, and for Newbie Lodge, craftsman Magnus Vistaunet was the building contractor and J. F. K. Messerschmidt was the painter. The results speak for themselves; the grand reception hall opens up to a second storey with a

~ 1015 East Island Highway ~

balcony surrounding it, a typical Maclure feature. The hall is dominated by a large fireplace.

For the next decade the long, winding gravel driveway leading to the lodge saw many comings and goings as the Beatties lavishly entertained the local gentry. Their company arrived in buggies, on horseback or even in the latest automobiles of the day. It was the Roaring Twenties when people were dancing the Black Bottom and the Charleston and living in a carefree world after the horrors of World War I. Retired British military men and their wives, as well as most of the local socialites, frequented the lodge for dinner parties and soireés. The Chinese cook who worked for the Beatties became famous on the island for his gourmet dishes, and the tennis courts and rose gardens were appreciated. Certainly the lavish home of the Beatties was very popular with the elite of the day and was rivalled in size and grandeur only by General Money's home at Qualicum Beach. Through the years, visitors to the lodge included author Rudyard Kipling and actress Faye Wray, who became famous for her role in the original *King Kong* movie.

In 1929 Matthew Beattie, like many other businessmen and investors, lost a great deal of money in the Wall Street stock-market crash and during the Depression. In 1931 he was forced to sell Newbie Lodge and he and his wife left Vancouver Island for England, where they eventually amassed another fortune. However, they never returned to Canada.

Newbie Lodge was then bought by Commander Ernest May, an American naval officer who renamed it "Mayfields." Until 1942 it was the Mays' summer home. That year the property was purchased by Mr. and Mrs. David Charters of Bermuda, who opened the acreage as a fancy summer guesthouse resort under the name of "Beach Acres." By 1948 it was well established as a holiday resort, and more small cottages were built on the property so families could visit and enjoy the warm summer weather. At one point the lodge itself was converted into an Italian restaurant. In 1958 Beach Acres became the property of Mr. and Mrs. B. Ellis and Mr. and Mrs. T. Groves, who added still more cottages along the beachfront and in the forest.

By the 1980s the declining economy had taken its toll on Beach Acres and the grand Maclure house. The beautiful grounds and the cottages were in desperate need of maintenance and upkeep, and for a while the resort closed down as the lodge became the subject of a heritage-conservation study to decide its worth. Meanwhile developers debated the fate of the surrounding Beach Acres Resort. In 1981, the entire property was sold to some Alberta oilmen and there were rumours that luxury condominiums would be built on the property. Lack of a local sewer system put an end to those plans.

Then, in 1986, a development company purchased the land and strata-titled the acreage into 75 lots. This was the first arrangement of its kind on Vancouver Island. The vacation homes were all to be privately owned with owners having the option to either participate in a rental pool and receive an income, or simply use their cottage as a year-round getaway.

The grand opening of the new Beach Acres Resort took place in May 1987 and further development occurred in five phases. In phases 1 and 2, over 24 of the beachfront cottages were completed, with recreation facilities including barbecue areas, tennis courts, shuffleboard court, playgrounds and picnic shelters. A further 18 homes were also nearing completion. Phases 3, 4 and 5 included more vacation homes in the forest, plus a recreation centre, indoor swimming pool and meeting and banquet rooms. The new resort was the dream of Andrew and Susan Pearson, who organized its development.

Newbie Lodge itself is now maintained as the Maclure House Inn and Restaurant by Michael and Penny McBride, the owners since 1992. They have endeavoured to keep the lodge true to its original heritage and era. It has been lovingly maintained and the McBrides still greet guests from all over the world with old-world charm reminiscent of the days of Matthew and Evelyn Beattie.

In 1997 Beach Acres Resort was voted Hotel of the Year by the Northwest Commercial Travellers' Association, and in 1999 readers of *Beautiful British Columbia Magazine* recognized Beach Acres as 11th among favourite resorts in British Columbia.

Situated on the sunny shores of the Strait of Georgia with beaches that stretch more than half a mile out toward Mistaken Island at low tide, Beach Acres Resort and the Maclure House Inn and Restaurant offer relaxing, peaceful getaways that combine country ambience and modern-day luxury.

TAMARACK HOUSE

From Chicken Farm to Bed and Breakfast

In 1912 the Golding family arrived in Qualicum from Saskatchewan, purchased acreage that had formed most of Qualicum Woods and became pioneer settlers. Before coming, Charles and Mary Golding ordered a two-storey house through the mail from Sears-Roebuck. Their pre-fabricated house arrived in Qualicum by train.

Today it is hard to imagine Sears selling houses, especially ones that could be shipped and then assembled on site, but Richard Sears, a railroad agent and watch salesman, offered many people this opportunity in 1908 and continued to do so through the popular Sears catalogue for some years. Sears and his partner, repairman Alvah Roebuck, had formed their company in 1886 but Roebuck sold out in 1895, and Sears went on alone to achieve great wealth and fame in the following years.

The Goldings and their six children lived on their land in tents until their house arrived and was assembled. Charles Golding grew impatient waiting for the house to be completed so once the roof was on, he moved his family in, even though there were still no windows or doors. That same night a heavy snowfall caused their two tents to collapse.

The home was eventually completed, and the Goldings settled in and began raising chickens on their farm. Their day-old chicks were sold to places as far away as China. The eggs were also sold to local residents, and their roasters and fryers were popular with everyone, especially the local hotels. Golding chickens soon became well known throughout the entire island. The family raised thousands each year and the children recall selling roast chicken on the beach to tourists, as well as spending a great deal of time washing eggs. Every Sunday morning they roasted about a dozen chickens, which they then sold to campers for 25 cents apiece.

In those early days, one of the barns on the Goldings' acreage also served as a temporary Anglican Church; their involvement in the community was apparent in many areas.

Mary Golding was the fourth child, and she became an important figure in the Qualicum area. As a child, she attended the Qualicum Beach Public School (now the Old School House) and in 1922, at age 15, she obtained her Grade 8 diploma. In 1927 she married Russ Hayes, who operated PDQ Trucking in Qualicum, and they lived in a house behind the site of the present Canadian

~ 568 Tamarack Drive ~

Imperial Bank of Commerce. In 1931, Mary and Russ and their children moved to Powell River where Russ worked at the pulp mill. Later he opened Russ Hayes Service, a gas station and automobile repair business. When Russ joined the air force in World War II, Mary ran this business.

After the war, Russ sold gas-manufacturing power plants up and down the coast and then became a pump-station operator for Trans Mountain Pipeline. He died suddenly in 1959, and Mary decided to move back to Qualicum Beach, where many of her siblings were still living. Her father, Charles, had died in 1939, and her mother, Mary, in 1959, and after this the chicken farm and old house were sold. During Mary's years back in Qualicum, she became a well-respected member of St. Stephen's United Church.

In 1966, Mary remarried. She and her husband, Ed Putland, lived on West Crescent Road until early 1998, and in September of that year she passed away at the grand age of 91. She was survived by her daughter Doreen and son Gordon.

In 1998, the Golding farmhouse became the home of Brenda and Henk Witmans, who converted it into a charming bed and breakfast. Because its address is 568 Tamarack Drive, it was called "Tamarack House," but the choice was appropriate for quite another reason. The tamarack tree is a member of the pine and larch family with flaky, dark reddish-gray bark that resembles the black spruce. The tamarack tree has a strong historical connection to the First Nations peoples because its dried, hard wood was good for making shelters and tools. The inner bark of the tamarack was also once used for medicinal purposes, but its most appropriate connection to Tamarack House today comes from the fact that hunters once used the ground around the tamarack tree as a resting place in spring and summer, just as travellers in the 21st century might use Tamarack House today.

LONG DISTANCE

Veronica's House Was Fit for Royalty

There is a certain mystique about the Milner Estate and Gardens just off the highway leading into Qualicum Beach. The 40-acre property includes the Milner house, named "Long Distance" by its late owner, socialite Veronica Milner, and a woodland garden paradise that she created over four decades.

The house was started in 1929 and completed in 1931 for Hilda Bayley, the sister of General Noel Money, and Hilda and Noel's mother, Emily Louisa Money, both of whom had moved to Qualicum Beach in 1929. General Money was the man who put Qualicum on the map. After coming to Vancouver Island on a fishing trip in 1913, he bought a number of lots, on many of which he built.

The house for his sister and mother was first known simply as "the cottage for Mrs. Bayley" and was designed much in the style of a Ceylonese tea-plantation house (an understandable choice, since the Bayleys had once owned a tea plantation in Ceylon). Its bungalow style — complete with a large outside veranda to accommodate potted plants, cane furniture and blinds — was more conducive to life on a tea plantation than to a waterfront cottage on Vancouver

Island. Each bedroom had its own bathroom (an unusual feature for a 1930s house), and each bathroom had a screened door leading to the outside, allowing servants to enter and run a bath without disturbing the sleeping occupant.

Due to Mrs. Money's ill health, Hilda Bayley and her mother only lived in the "cottage" for a short time. The property was too large for them, so it was put up for sale. Around this time, Horatio Ray Milner, KC, and his wife, Rina, were visiting Qualicum.

Ray Milner was an astute businessman born in 1889 in Sackville, New Brunswick, into a United Empire Loyalist family. After graduating from Dalhousie University in 1911, he was called to the bar and began his career, but not initially in law. There was not a great call for lawyers in the Maritimes and, because of a bronchial condition Ray had had since childhood, an aunt advised him to head west where opportunities abounded and the weather was better. He arrived in Edmonton with only $75 to his name during a peak period in industry and population expansion. When World War I broke out, Ray Milner joined the Edmonton Fusiliers, despite his health problems.

~ 2179 West Island Highway ~

While hospitalized in England, he met Catherine "Rina" Bury, a woman with whom he had been enamoured back in Edmonton. She was much older than he was and at the time had been married, though separated from her husband. Now she was nursing in England and a free woman, and Ray fell in love all over again. The couple were married upon Ray's demobilization in 1919, and in 1921 he was named King's Counsel at the young age of 32. Milner's career then took off, as he became legal advisor to Prime Minister R. B. Bennett and travelled to London to argue before the Privy Council on behalf of the Province of Saskatchewan.

In 1932 he became president of Northwestern Utilities, Canadian Western and Canadian Western Utilities. The wealthier Ray Milner became, however, the more he considered his fellow man, giving his money away to those less fortunate and to numerous charities. He never forgot his early hardships, and was especially noted for his years of service to such organizations as the Salvation Army, the Canadian National Institute for the Blind and the Edmonton Community Chest.

By 1937 Ray and Rina Milner were looking for a summer place where they could escape from the business world. They chose Qualicum Beach, where many other Edmonton businessmen had summer houses. By then, they also had a daughter who had polio and they were told the climate in Qualicum would be good for her. On April 14, 1937, the property now known as the Milner Estate became theirs.

They used the estate primarily in the summer but also spent many spring and Thanksgiving holidays at the property. Rina lived there more than her world-travelling husband and established the house as a warm and welcoming retreat for friends and family. She also began to take a great interest in the surrounding garden and woodlands. Slowly the estate took shape under her dedicated touch.

Sad to say, Rina was suffering from a hereditary illness and was ill for about 12 years before finally passing away in November 1952. Ray was devastated by his loss and by 1953, ". . . the gardens, and Ray, were at a crossroads. . ." wrote Margaret Cadwaldr in her book *In Veronica's Garden.* But things did not remain that way for long. Through his friend Colonel Bourke, Ray had been introduced to Ted and Mary Greig, from whom he began to order plants, and with their assistance and excellent advice, the grounds slowly became "more highly refined."

But the greatest change for both Ray Milner and his estate was yet to come. He would soon meet Veronica, widow of Desmond Windham Otho Fitzgerald, the 28th Knight of Glin Castle, County Limerick, in Ireland, and life at the Milner Estate would never be quite the same again.

Veronica Villiers Fitzgerald was born in London, England, in 1909, into the aristocracy. She was once quoted as saying of herself, "I am not important. My importance is only because I was associated with important people." She was indeed connected to and surrounded by "important people" all her life. The Villiers were a long-standing family of note in England. Veronica's mother was a cousin of Winston Churchill; she was descended from the Duke of Marlborough and related to Diana Spencer, Princess of Wales. One of Veronica's ancestors, Barbara Villiers, was mistress to King Charles II.

Veronica was proud of her colourful ancestry, but had spent a lonely and unhappy childhood, during which her passions were art and gardening. Her somewhat dysfunctional early family life (splendidly recorded in Cadwaladr's book), led Veronica into an early marriage in January 1929, a month before her 20th birthday, to Desmond Fitzgerald. After a honeymoon in Europe, the couple returned to take up residence at Glin Castle.

Life with an overpowering father-in-law and an unfriendly housekeeper, and the knowledge that the Fitzgeralds' dwindling fortunes were making the future of Glin uncertain at best, meant a difficult existence for the young, inexperienced bride. It also did not bode well for a happy marriage, mainly because Veronica was headstrong and often unpleasant, and Desmond had many health problems. The only things they had in common were their love of the gardens of Glin and their many dogs. Desmond passed away in 1949, leaving Veronica with three children and little money. But she did have a son, and that meant Glin could be saved. Veronica was determined that the 29th Knight of Glin would inherit his birthright and that Glin Castle and his estate would thrive once more.

Ray Milner first met Veronica in the United States when she was on a trip with Desmond trying to restore his failing health. When Ray renewed his relationship with her in her widowhood, he fell in love with this vivacious woman. At the time he was in his 60s and she was 45. Some people said Veronica was attracted to Ray because he was rich — and maybe they were partly right. However, this strong-willed, determined lady also had great respect for Ray Milner and grew to love him in her own way. They were married in London in 1954 with Veronica dressed, perhaps symbolically in keeping with her erratic nature, in a fiery red dress.

The marriage, however, proved to be a salvation not only for Glin Castle, into which Ray Milner generously poured a great deal of his money, but also for his Qualicum estate to which Veronica moved with her new husband. She felt somewhat isolated there — her reason for calling the house "Long Distance" — and she could not adjust to the Canadian way of life. As it had been ingrained into her from birth to consider herself a little better than others, her attitude often caused her to be at odds with people. Very few people were considered her friends and fewer still tried to understand this often-outrageous woman. She did not suffer fools gladly and made her opinions known to one and all, often at the expense of someone's feelings.

She did, however, have a vision for the Milner Estate, which she put into practice through the years, transforming the wooded acres into a magical retreat leading to a country garden amidst towering Douglas firs and cedars. Nursery operators Ted and Mary Greig again assisted with advice on rhododendrons and various other plants. Over 500 varieties of rhododendron were planted to separate the forest from the garden. Veronica wished to preserve the estate as a sanctuary and her idea of a garden style had "an artistic sensibility and vagueness

to it." Where grass grew long, paths were mown beneath the trees. People, she thought, should come to the estate for "renewal and inspiration."

Princess Diana and Prince Charles chose the Milner estate to escape to for a few hours while in Canada for their Expo '86 tour. They both wrote charming letters to Veronica afterwards, thanking her for her kind hospitality and the sense of freedom they had experienced there. Prince Charles spent a few hours painting watercolours in the grounds, and Diana remarked on how much she enjoyed the casual smorgasbord dining. A photograph of her in the dining room shows her perched on a chair with her plate on her lap, in animated conversation. This was at the time when she was said to have numerous eating disorders.

The following year Her Majesty Queen Elizabeth and Prince Philip stayed at the Milner Estate for a few days of relaxation. On that occasion Veronica graciously consented to move out so the Queen and her staff could enjoy complete privacy. The Queen agreed to plant a tree on the estate in honour of their visit. Prince Philip wandered the grounds with his camera casually slung around his neck, as he captured the beauty of this island paradise on film. The simplicity of their adjoining bedrooms would have been in strong contrast to life in a palace or castle.

Ray Milner died at his home in Qualicum on May 24, 1975, at the age of 86 and was buried in Edmonton near his first wife, Rina. Veronica carried on with her vision for the estate and many say she became more disagreeable and impossible as she aged. Often at dinner parties she would thump her hand on the table and say, "I have spoken!" Her word was not to be disputed. The very few who did become close to her respected her as a friend – if she liked you, you were valued in return. One such person was Margaret Cadwaladr, the author of her story.

Margaret is the wife of Jim Cadwaladr, now the executive director of the Milner Gardens. In 1996, Veronica gave her home and surrounding gardens to Malaspina College in memory of Ray Milner. She had worried that with the failing economy and her finances slowly depleting, the Milner Estate would eventually have to be sold. Instead, because of her generosity, it is now a regional facility used extensively by horticulture students at Malaspina University College, under Jim Cadwaladr's guidance. The garden has received much attention around the world, including from the American Association of Botanical Gardens and Arboreta, which advised the board of directors on the further development of Veronica's vision.

A large part of the forest is still old growth, and once a visitor has passed through this wilderness, the landscape opens to the 10-acre garden oasis with its manicured lawns and spectacular views of the Strait of Georgia, islands and the Sunshine Coast. The estate is now open to the public throughout the summer.

The Milner estate has become far more than just a house with a garden in the woods. As one walks through the paths among acres of towering trees leading up to the house itself, one can sense that touch of magic Veronica created. At first simply a vision, eventually it became a reality, and now the estate has become a fitting monument to Veronica Milner, an often-eccentric lady who was certainly a little different from the rest.

Veronica Villiers Fitzgerald Milner passed away at the age of 89 in 1998. After her Qualicum funeral, some of her ashes were spread by her son, Desmond, in the grounds of the Milner Estate. The rest he took back to Glin in Ireland to spread in her "Irish garden." A pair of her secateurs was buried in the family graveyard at St. Paul's Church near Glin Castle.

ROSEMUIR

Qualicum's First Designated Heritage House

The house known as "Rosemuir" on West Crescent Avenue in Qualicum Beach was built in 1928 by A. N. Fraser as a summer home for the Pinkard family from New York. It has a steep shake roof and a 30- by-20-foot living room with a cathedral ceiling. Two beams span the ceiling for support.

This delightful home with a long history was awarded heritage designation in May 1993, the first residence in the area to receive such an honour. A building plaque from the Town of Qualicum Beach was presented to the owners, and more than 30 people witnessed Mayor Jack Collins affix the plaque to the wall beside the front door.

The owners at that time, sisters Hallie Muir and Alice-Jean MacKay, initiated the heritage-designation process for the house. It seemed to them that this piece of old Qualicum needed to be preserved. The sisters had named the house, which held many happy memories for them, by combining the family name, Muir, with the roses that always grew abundantly in the garden.

A few years earlier, when the Muir sisters had tried to sell the house and the 2.7-acre property surrounding it, which included another small house and cabin, no one seemed interested in buying it as a complete unit. Many developers, however, wished to subdivide the property, which the sisters did not want to do, so they took it off the market. They then approached the Town of Qualicum Beach, asking how their property could be preserved. The heritage conservation department became involved, as did Councillor Brian Dietrich and Jim Storey, president of the Qualicum Beach Historical and Museum Society.

Once Rosemuir was granted heritage-building status, future owners of the property would be obliged to maintain the buildings and the surrounding forest and gardens in their entirety: changes could only be made with the permission and approval of the Town of Qualicum Beach. The sisters were happy with the arrangement because the acreage included two large redwood trees that had been planted when the house was built, as well as a much older Douglas fir where eagles continued to roost.

Everyone agreed that the Muirs' house itself had exceptional character. During World War II, the Muirs had held a number of fundraising events there for the Red Cross. The grounds were also well used through the years for wedding photographs.

~ 246 West Crescent Road ~

The historical importance of Rosemuir dates back even further than the time the house was built. The acreage was part of the original 1913 subdivision owned by General Noel Money. At that time many other houses were being built in the area including Major Lowery's Log House on East Crescent, General Money's own house (now known as the Brown House) and Valhalla.

With their home now protected by its heritage designation, the Muir sisters were able to sell their property to a couple from California and move with other family members to Texada Island, knowing that Rosemuir and its acreage would be left in peace for future generations to enjoy.

VALHALLA

The White House with Medical Connections

Like many heritage homes in the Qualicum Beach area, 210 West Crescent Road was built in 1912. It was intended for the first manager of the Qualicum Beach Inn and golf course, Thompson Tinn. Other sources claim that the house was built for one of the contractors of the hotel, a Mr. Humphrey. In the beginning, it was known as the "White House," because of its colour and not because of any connection to the famous home of the same name in Washington, D.C.

During World War I, the Qualicum Beach Inn was turned into a convalescent home for wounded officers and the White House became a nurses' residence. Dr. Campbell Davidson was in charge of the hospital, and he and his wife and the nurses held many parties in the White House to help keep up the spirits of the officers. In one sad story, a nurse fell in love with an officer who did not return her affection, so the unfortunate young woman hanged herself in the doorway of one of the larger back bedrooms of the house. Many subsequent owners of the house claim to have seen her ghostly presence, so the story has continued and has sometimes been embellished over the years.

Once the war was over, both the inn and the White House reverted to their original states and life returned to normal. The White House then had many owners, the first being the Morgan family, who lived there during 1919 and 1920. They found the house unpleasantly cold, but were relieved to find that the nurses had left behind plenty of coal to keep it warm. The nurses had also left numerous cats that roamed everywhere, a not-so-pleasant discovery.

In those days the large living room was panelled, with an ornamental plate rail circling the walls, which the Morgans painted green. Later occupants repainted them a lighter colour. There was a beamed ceiling and a large fireplace with a five-foot opening which could easily accommodate a four-foot log.

Later owners were the Kennedys, followed by the Havemeyer family. Mr. Havemeyer was a very large man, but all 6 feet 7 inches of him could easily fit into the magnificent bathtub installed in the original bathroom, described by subsequent owners as "a swimming pool." The Havemeyer's daughter owned a Shetland pony that she brought inside the house on cold winter nights so that he could lie in front of the fireplace and enjoy the warmth.

— 210 West Crescent Road —

The McGivern family also lived in the White House for a while, as did General Money, owner of the Qualicum Beach Inn, while waiting for his own house to be completed.

In 1941 Mr. and Mrs. Knight purchased the house and set about restoring it. They lived there happily for 15 years, during which time they painted, added a second bathroom and installed central heating. Through those years life in the house was always busy with their own five children and many friends dropping by.

In 1956 the house was sold to the Battens, but Mr. Batten died within a year and the house was sold yet again to Min and Bill Murray. The next owner, Mrs. Jill Proctor, removed the dark panelling and plate rail in the living room, giving her more room to display her large collection of antiques in a brighter area.

When Mrs. Proctor passed away, the house was sold to Reg and Lillian Dill. The Dills renamed the house "Valhalla," the name they had called all their former homes. In keeping with the Dills' wishes, the house was eventually bequeathed to the Town of Qualicum Beach and later became the offices for the Canadian Cancer Society, with a view to its becoming a hospice.

The word Valhalla, according to ancient Norse mythology, means the final resting place for brave and noble Vikings, where good food, music and friendships were shared. In view of Valhalla's history, it seems a most fitting name, rounding off the medical connection the house has had since World War I, when wounded officers were also cared for in a most amenable resting place.

BROWN HOUSE

Protecting Colonel Money's Qualicum Estate

Once referred to as the "Qualicum Mansion" for its opulence, this property on East Crescent Road was later called the Brown House. It took its name not from its colour, but from the Brown family who were residents.

The story begins at the time of the early settlement of Qualicum Beach in 1910, following the extension of the Esquimalt & Nanaimo Railway north from Nanaimo to Courtenay. A land boom ensued when H. E. Beasley, a railway official, sponsored a land development company known as the Merchants Trust and Trading Company which purchased a great deal of land from the railway company. The centre of this property was where Memorial Avenue is today. The company, hoping to entice people to settle there, began building a hotel and golf course in 1913 and offered the remaining land as private residential lots.

In 1913 Noel Money, born in Montreal and educated in England, visited Qualicum Beach on a fishing trip. Money had already had a distinguished career, having served in India and receiving the South Africa medal during the Boer War. While he was in Qualicum he slept on the floor of the unfinished Qualicum Beach Inn, and

wrote in his journal, ". . . spent 10 days in Qualicum Beach and bought six lots." The purchase of the 6 lots, totalling 55 acres, was arranged through Thompson Tinn, managing director of the Merchants Trust and Trading Company and later the first manager of the Qualicum Beach Inn and golf course. The two men agreed that Money would return to England to settle his affairs there, then bring his family back to Qualicum, where he would take over as managing director and run the hotel. The Moneys returned in February 1914 and lived in Tinn's house (now known as Valhalla) while their own home was being built on East Crescent Road. It was to become the largest and most prestigious home in Qualicum.

Eventually Money raised the funds to buy the Qualicum Beach Inn and the golf course himself, but before that he returned to England to resume his military career at the outbreak of World War I. He distinguished himself as a hero while commanding the 159th Welsh Division during the capture of the Mount of Olives in Jerusalem in 1917.

Now named General Money, he returned to Qualicum in 1919 to reside in his "mansion" and to open

~ East Crescent Road ~

the Qualicum Beach Inn in grand style. Many famous people visited the hotel through the years, including Errol Flynn, Shirley Temple, Bob Hope and Bing Crosby.

Noel Money managed the hotel, golf course and acreage where his own house stood until his death in 1941 at age 74. His next-door neighbour, Major Lowery, then purchased the house and land and held it until 1952, when it was sold to Calgary lawyer and board member of Home Oil, R. A. "Bobby" Brown. From then on the house was always referred to as the Brown House. The Brown family lived in the house for two decades before Bobby Brown passed away in 1971, leaving the golf course, the 55 acres and other assets in trust. The major beneficiary was his wife, Genevieve Brown.

In 1981 the Town of Qualicum Beach purchased the golf course from the family trust for a million dollars. Meanwhile, the house and the parcel of land which surrounds it remained a prized piece of real estate. The land was considered to have the finest surviving original forest on the east coast of Vancouver Island. Its trees ranged from newly planted saplings to 500- and 600-year-old giants. In addition, coho-bearing Beach Creek ran through the property.

In 1996 the Brown Family Trust approached the Town of Qualicum Beach with a developer's plan for a subdivision of 110 lots on the Brown property, a plan which would remove all the trees on the 50 acres, except "where not permitted by legislation that protects the riparian zone of Beach Creek." The remaining five-acre parcel, which included the house itself, a pool, cabana, tennis court and garden, was excluded from the plan.

As a result of this proposal, the Brown Property Preservation Society was quickly formed to protect the valuable property. The five acres were bought by a development group and resold to another group that plans to turn the house into a hotel while retaining the acreage.

Meanwhile, the Brown Property Preservation Society is still working to preserve the remaining 50 acres as a wilderness park with signs and pathways for citizens to enjoy. So far, everyone who wanders through the acreage has respected its heritage and helped to keep it clean. Fundraising continues in order to ensure that this important heritage site will eventually be turned over to the Town of Qualicum for future stewardship.

COURTENAY, COMOX AND CUMBERLAND

The first inhabitants of the Comox Valley were the Coast Salish; European settlers arrived in 1862. Sixty people were sent by the Hudson's Bay Company to farm the area, and in 1863, when coal was discovered on the Tsable River, the first mine went into operation. In 1864 the community of Union was founded after coal was also discovered in the Cumberland area.

The town of Cumberland came into being in 1889 and was incorporated a mere nine years later. Cumberland was given its name because many of the miners were from Cumberland in England. The Chinese population in Cumberland once equalled that of San Francisco's Chinatown. Cumberland remained an active coal-mining town until the 1960s, surviving devastating mine explosions and many labour disputes. The Cumberland Museum is filled with artifacts recalling this colourful mining past.

In 1910 the Comox Logging and Railway Company was formed, and for a brief period it was the largest logging company in the British Empire. The entire Comox Valley has a rich heritage in the logging industry. In 1942 a Canadian Forces Base was opened in Comox as a strategic defence location, and this air base has been at the centre of life in the community ever since.

The name Comox is from the word *Komuckyway* meaning "plenty" or "abundance," referring to the abundance of game and berries in the area. Comox was also once known as Port Augusta.

The town of Courtenay was laid out in 1891 and named for the nearby Courtenay River, itself named in 1860 for Captain George William Courtenay of the HMS *Constance*.

The three houses in this section include one built in 1912 for the early pioneering Duncan family; another built in 1918 for Major Hilton, a logging company owner; and, finally, the famous Filberg Lodge, with its delightful surrounding park in Comox.

Their stories will be revealed as we continue our journey north.

SANDWICK MANOR

The Faux-Stone House with a Friendly Ghost

In 1862 William Duncan was one of the first pioneers in the Comox Valley. Duncan kept a detailed journal on early life in the valley. He was enchanted by the New World and obviously sent word of its merits to his family back home, for on June 20, 1877, his nephew Eric Duncan arrived from Scotland. Eric, then a young man of 19, soon became equally impressed with the landscape at Comox Landing.

At first he worked on the Robb farm, where for 10 hours of labour he could earn two dollars. Back in Scotland, Eric had only made the equivalent of 50 cents for 12 hours of work, so it was hardly surprising that he thought he had landed in Utopia. The Robb family had arrived on Vancouver Island in 1862 aboard the famous *Tynemouth,* one of the bride ships. Mrs. Robb had acted as matron on the *Tynemouth* to the 60 female passengers sent to the colony as potential wives for the settlers.

The rest of Eric's family, including his brother William, arrived in 1880, and all settled happily in the valley. By then Eric had purchased 150 acres of his own land, which became known as the Duncan farm. His acreage started at the Courtenay River and extended to the top of Ryan Road.

Eric was a man of many talents — not only a farmer, but also an accomplished writer and poet. In addition he became the first postmaster for the young community, known at that time as Mission. When Eric applied to the federal government for the name of the postal outlet to be Mission officially, his request was rejected because there was already a community by that name on the mainland. He applied for the name Duncan, but again discovered that a settlement to the south on Vancouver Island had already taken that name. He then suggested the name Sandwick, his town back in the Shetland Islands, and this name was accepted. So it was that the community of Sandwick came into being.

In 1912 Eric built a large home for his wife Anna, himself and their adopted son, Charles, whose mother, a Mrs. Pritchard, had died giving birth to Charles and his twin brother, Norman, in the early 1890s. Eric called their house "Sandwick Manor."

Charles was killed during World War I, and Anna, who suffered from severe arthritis, died in 1920. By 1925 Eric felt he could no longer live alone in Sandwick Manor, a house that needed a family to enjoy its spaciousness. He decided to sell it to Norman, the other Pritchard twin.

~ 276 Sandwick Road ~

Norman Pritchard then farmed the land and lived in the house until the early 1930s, at which time the Depression hit and he lost the farm to the local creamery co-operative. For the next few years, the co-op rented the house to their employees. They also split up the acreage and sold off many portions. Ten lots on the east side had Veterans Land Act (VLA) homes built on them for veterans returning from World War II.

In the early 1940s the Campbell family purchased the house and property and ran a very successful chicken farm for many years. In 1964 Art Leakey purchased the three remaining acres and the house. His son, Edwin, took over the property in 1967 and lived there for a number of years. In 1979 two more acres were sold, this time to the federal government for a local RCMP station.

Today Kim Sleno, Edwin Leakey's second wife, still lives in the house, with her husband Charlie Sallis. Kim is the longest-term resident of Sandwick Manor to date, having lived in the house for over 26 years.

This claim may not be totally true because a ghost, affectionately known as "Aunt Anna," has been added to the list of occupants of Sandwick Manor. Aunt Anna's presence has been felt in the house since 1938, approximately 18 years after a woman of that name died, but the only people who have actually seen her were both 12-year-old girls, one in 1938 and the other in 1998. Kim, however, believes she has experienced Aunt Anna's pranks in the house on many occasions. Her husband, Charlie, who generally does not believe in such paranormal activity, did admit that one night he saw a "misty glow" that quickly disappeared in the spare bedroom. The animals in the house seem to sense Aunt Anna's presence more than people do. Often, Kim and Charlie's two dogs, one cat and a bird all stare together at one particular spot on the ceiling, and yet no one can see anything there.

Kim and Charlie have extensively renovated Sandwick Manor over the years but have managed to retain the old world amid the modern conveniences. They have also created a wonderful garden on their acreage, featuring large rhododendrons and fruit trees planted well over 80 years ago when the Duncan acreage stretched for miles.

Sandwick Manor is built entirely of faux stone, or concrete-block forms created to look like granite. These forms were purchased by Eric Duncan from Samuel Cotton, who owned the block company; they were brought from Vancouver and erected on the site by Cotton. The slate roof came from Scotland and was transported to Canada around Cape Horn. Many other features in the house, including the gingerbread work on the front of the house, the fir stairway with its eight-inch newel post, and the oak mantelpiece in the living room, were purchased from a Sears Roebuck catalogue.

Kim Sleno is proud of her manor house, which today remains an important part of the Comox Valley heritage.

GREYSTONE MANOR

A Manor House Built for a Lumber Baron

This beautiful heritage home, one of the oldest in the Comox Valley, sits well back from the highway in Royston. It was built in 1918 for Major and Mrs. Hilton, and has a view of Comox Bay and the mainland coastal mountains. Married in 1911, the Hiltons first lived in Courtenay, where Major Hilton started the Bevan Mill. This mill cut the lumber used in building his house. His architect was a man named Owen and the house was built by Jack Irwin and Bert Knappett. Later alterations were made by Mr. A. W. Rigler.

In 1921 the house was ready for the Hiltons and their three children, and, appropriately, they called their home "Hilton House." The spacious grounds required a great deal of work, so they employed a Chinese gardener to take care of the vegetable garden, fruit trees and rose arbour. He was then allowed to sell any extra produce from the garden for his own spending money. In 1929, Major Hilton closed down his logging company to retire, and his oldest son, Jack, took over the market-garden business to support his family.

In April 1936, Hilton House was saved from major fire damage by the quick action of the Courtenay Fire Brigade, which used its new pumper truck for the first time. One Sunday night, while reading in bed, Major Hilton was disturbed by a strange noise that he could not recognize. Looking around, he found nothing amiss so he continued reading until two o'clock, when he finally fell asleep. Two hours later he was awakened once again by an unfamiliar noise, so he decided to go through the entire house this time; he still could find nothing wrong. Then, glancing out of a window, he saw the reflection of a bright glow coming from the house. He ran outside to discover that the corner of the roof was alight and the fire spreading rapidly. At a quarter to five, he called in an alarm which was answered by Muriel Leighton, the operator on duty at the fire station. Within ten minutes the Courtenay Fire Brigade had made the four-mile journey to the house and quickly smothered the roof with water from their 200-gallon pumper truck. The flames were contained by the enormous pressure, so very little water had to be used and only minor damage was done. A few rafters and about two thousand shingles had to be replaced, but Major Hilton was convinced that had the brigade not responded so promptly and had the pumper truck not been in operation, the entire house would have been destroyed. It was concluded that the fire had

135

~ 4014 Haas Road ~

probably started when a spark from the chimney landed on the roof.

In 1959 the house was sold to Herbert and Pat Thompson. Originally Hilton House had been covered with clapboard, but in 1961 it was one of the first houses in the Comox Valley to be stuccoed. The Thompsons stayed until 1980, when the house was bought by Frank and Joan Dye. It changed ownership yet again in 1985 when Mary Nelson and Cathy and Bruce Stringer purchased it and opened it as a bed and breakfast for the first time. Mary decided to change the name to "Greystone Manor" on the advice of relatives who thought that name suited it better.

On a visit from Bath, England, in the 1980s, current owners Maureen and Mike Shipton suddenly decided that they wanted to move to Canada. Their three earlier holiday visits had convinced them that the Comox Valley was the place for them. They applied to emigrate; by the end of September 1990 they were back in the valley with two suitcases; the remainder of their belongings and furniture were on their way via the Panama Canal. They had no idea what they wanted to do in Canada, so for a while they stayed with relatives in Royston. Five weeks later they noticed that the Greystone Manor bed and breakfast was for sale; the house was everything they had been looking for.

Once they moved in, however, they realized there was much work to be done. Wallpaper festooned with large sunflower designs hung on some of the walls, the ceiling paint was flaking and certain areas of the house were dark. One of the bedrooms had a strange odour which, once the plywood had been removed from the walls, turned out to be due to dampness around the window; the wood there had completely rotted. That whole window had to be replaced, and this was the first stage in some major renovations.

A second storey, in keeping with the original character of the house, was added, and the Shiptons have also included their own touches through the years. The original hardwood floors in the dining room, hall and living room were exposed when carpet or lino dating from the 1960s was taken up. The gleaming wood panelling in the dining room and living room had remained intact, as had the wooden plate racks and window seats.

Today the house, which is over 3,000 square feet in size, features solid double windows and improved floors that better retain the heat from the old-fashioned, water-filled, oil-fired radiators. There are five bedrooms and a so-called maid's room that has sloping ceilings and overlooks the lawn and garden. The lack of heat in the maid's room is a sign of bygone times when it was considered a luxury to heat servants' quarters!

The original bathroom, once the only one in the house, still has a claw-foot tub and a laundry chute to the basement. Two new bathrooms have been added.

The dining room contains a beautiful Victorian dining table with a Welsh-slate base. Underneath its highly polished mahogany surface can be found a billiard table for after-dinner billiard matches. The sunken living room off the dining room was added by the Shiptons for their own private enjoyment.

The delightful English flower gardens created by the Shiptons, with views across Comox Bay to the mountains, are enjoyed by all the guests who stay at Greystone Manor today. The Shiptons have added many old-world English garden touches throughout the acreage.

Mo Shipton says, "It is fortunate that the property was not cleared of all the old trees surrounding it. There are still four old horse chestnuts, several Douglas firs, a Garry oak and two native dogwoods." The manor house is also close to the famous Royston Wrecks, rusting old hulks of various boats sunk approximately 40 years ago to form a breakwater for log booms. The wrecks are of considerable historic interest to sightseers, as is the Comox Logging railway track that is now a public walkway.

Guests from around the world stay at Greystone Manor to enjoy its beauty and air of peaceful relaxation. Many keep returning, obviously entranced by the tranquility created by an English couple from Bath who cherish the home whose heritage they have restored.

FILBERG LODGE

A Rustic Paradise

Near the end of Comox Avenue in the town of Comox is the estate and former home of Robert J. Filberg and his wife, Florence McCormack Filberg. Today the lodge and nine acres of beautiful landscaped grounds are a public facility run by the Filberg Lodge and Park Association; this non-profit society manages the grounds on behalf of the municipality.

Robert Filberg came to British Columbia as a young man in 1909 and soon made his mark and fortune in the logging industry. He became an influential person in the Comox Valley, acting as president and director of many logging operations there, including the Comox Logging and Railway Company, the Canadian Western Lumber Company and Crown Zellerbach.

By 1929 he and his wife decided to have master builder William Hagarty supervise the construction of a home on their acreage. The result was a delightful house nestled comfortably into the hillside overlooking the water. Much of the stonework on the building was completed by a stonemason who was later head gardener on the grounds, William Meier. Interestingly, the lodge's concrete foundation rests on piles driven into an old salt marsh and midden.

The inside of this beautiful, rustic lodge reflects the work of many talented local people. The best craftsmen in stone and timber worked on the house, creating a warm interior that complements the rustic, natural exterior. Many of the inside beams and much of the millwork was finished with an adze. The handrail on the staircase is crafted from a branching yew tree, and a First Nations petroglyph and a British Navy cannonball are cemented into the river-stone of the fireplace. The dining-room walls are finished in a rich honey-and-beeswax stain. All of this, as well as furniture from the 1800s and various curios collected by the Filbergs, give an impression of warmth and luxury. The bathroom is done in art-deco style, and numerous push-button bells are scattered throughout the lodge for the purpose, at one time, of summoning the servants.

The Filbergs lived in their charming home for many years, enjoying the good life while developing the grounds on their surrounding acreage. Mrs. Filberg had already passed away when Robert Filberg died in 1977 at the age of 87. He then donated his home and a multi-million-dollar trust fund to the

~ Comox Avenue ~

Vancouver Foundation, requesting that the interest from the fund be used to benefit the Comox Valley.

Alice Bullen, a councillor for the Town of Comox, then put forward to the Vancouver Foundation a request for a grant to purchase three acres and the Filberg house. The Vancouver Foundation agreed to grant the town $20,000 a year for 20 years to purchase the property and the lodge, plus another $20,000 a year for restoring the building and the grounds. As the Filbergs had not spent much time in Comox in the later years, preferring Hawaii in the winter, the property had become a part-time residence and was somewhat rundown.

Ten years after Robert Filberg's death, the Vancouver Foundation provided funds for purchase of the remaining six acres of the property, enabling the Filberg Lodge and Gardens to be brought back to their former beauty.

Today, under the management of the Filberg Lodge and Park Association, the gardens are a peaceful place to stroll among flowers, shrubs and trees (both exotic and local) and perhaps enjoy a picnic. During the summer, the Town of Comox also operates a farm featuring a variety of animals. A herb garden planted by the Comox Valley Horticultural Society is situated above the Tea House, which is open from May to September for morning coffee, lunches and afternoon teas. It occupies one of the restored outbuildings and is surrounded by a vine-covered patio. A recent addition to the grounds is the totem pole *Tla Wa Sints Guy U Las,* which means "strength of our ancestors." Designed and carved by Richard Krentz, it features Thunderbird, Sunman, White Whale (*Queneesh*) and Bear, the crests of the four main families of the Comox First Nation people. The totem pole was donated by Gordon and Ivy Wagner. It is located on an ancient First Nations midden and gazes seaward, thereby linking the valley with its native heritage.

Perhaps the most popular and well-known feature of the Filberg estate today is the annual Filberg Festival, which began in 1982 as the brainchild of Alice Bullen to create a place where artisans and craftspeople could show and sell their work. It has since become one of the best outdoor arts-and-crafts and music festivals on Vancouver Island. The festival is held in early August, but the park grounds are open year-round. The lodge itself is available for viewing at Easter and other weekends, as well as daily from June 1 to mid-September, and is well worth a visit.

In 2000, the grounds and lodge were granted heritage status. Many hours of dedicated volunteer work through the years have contributed to the great success of all the events that take place at the lodge and park.

The Filbergs would surely be delighted that their home has been put to such good use.

CAMPBELL RIVER AND THE NORTH ISLAND

Many people assume that Vancouver Island ends at Campbell River. In fact there is still much more of the Island to explore. This area is known as the North Island. Another 238 kilometres north of Campbell River lies Port Hardy at the end of Island Highway 19, and there is much to see in between these two towns. For those who prefer an even wilder and remote scenario, gravel roads and hiking trails lead to Cape Scott Provincial Park at the very tip of Vancouver Island.

Campbell River itself was named for Dr. Samuel Campbell, the surgeon on the HMS *Plumper,* a vessel that was used for mapping the coastline in the 19th century. Settlers began to arrive as logging camps were established. It was Sir Richard Musgrave who first wrote in a London journal about the abundant salmon in the area; this enticed people to come, and today Campbell River is still known as the "Salmon Capital of the World." Just as you are about to enter Campbell River you will notice on the waterfront a rock 30 feet high; some believe it's a remnant of the Ice Age. There is also a Native legend that a grizzly bear once claimed he could

jump from the mainland to Vancouver Island, but the tide was high and his back foot touched the water before he reached land on the island side. The Great Spirit, therefore, carried out his threat to turn the bear into stone for being too boastful – hence the "Big Rock."

An hour's drive west from Campbell River brings you to Gold River. It was incorporated on August 26, 1965, as a company town, and reincorporated on January 1, 1977. Gold River thrived on its surrounding timber resources and the construction of a mill. Once the pulp mill officially closed all operations in February 1999, the town with so much promise became something of a ghost town whose future still hangs in the balance.

One hour's drive north of Campbell River brings you to Sayward at the mouth of the Salmon River. First established as Port Kusum in the 1890s, it was renamed Salmon River in 1904 when the post office was installed there. In 1911, the town was officially named Sayward for William Parsons Sayward, a pioneer lumberman who never actually visited his namesake town. Sayward remained a remote logging community until after

World War II, when a gravel road (eventually paved) was finally put in from Campbell River.

Other small North Island communities include Woss, Zeballos, Tahsis, Alert Bay and Telegraph Cove, all with their own histories and personalities. In Zeballos the gold rush of the 1930s contributed to the style of buildings, such as the false-fronted stores and the Zeballos Hotel. In Telegraph Cove a community of waterfront buildings, many on pilings, reflects the cove's history of fishing and logging. The oldest buildings on the North Island are in Quatsino. St. Olaf's Anglican Church was built in 1896 and the Quatsino School celebrates its 100th anniversary in 2004. Eagle Manor, serving as a guesthouse today, was built there in 1912.

Farther north lie the communities of Port McNeill, Port Alice and Port Hardy. Port McNeill was named for Captain William Henry McNeill who worked for the Hudson's Bay Company at Fort Rupert, where a trading post had been established. He had captained the SS *Beaver*, the first steamship to operate along the west coast of British Columbia. The small community of Port Alice on Neroutsos Inlet is named for Alice Whalen, whose family operated three local pulp mills in the 1920s. In 1965 Port Alice became B.C.'s first instant municipality when a new town site was built to replace the company town.

Port Hardy, the largest community on the North Island, was named for Vice-Admiral Sir Thomas Masterman Hardy who captained the famous HMS *Victory*. At the Battle of Trafalgar he held the dying Lord Nelson in his arms. The first white settlers came to Port Hardy in the early 1900s; Alec and Sarah Lyon opened a store and post office on the east side of Hardy Bay in 1904. This was near the existing settlement of Fort Rupert, where First Nations culture has flourished for thousands of years.

Among the houses chosen for the North Island section are the Haig-Brown House in Campbell River, a little red house in Port McNeill belonging to a pioneer family named Betts, and one of the last houses in Port McNeill still standing where it was built by the Nippon Soda McNeill Trading Company in the 1930s. There are stories of some "alien" property, also in Port McNeill, and two Telegraph Cove houses with interesting tales.

Join me now as we conclude our tour of Vancouver Island's heritage homes.

HAIG-BROWN HOUSE

A Home, Museum, Education Centre and All Things Environmental

The Haig-Brown house, situated on the outskirts of Campbell River at 2250 Campbell River Road, was built in the 1920s. Roderick and Ann Haig-Brown became its owners in 1936. Surrounded by 20 acres of riverfront gardens and woodlands, it preserves Roderick Haig-Brown's memory as Vancouver Island's first conservationist. He was also a noted writer of works that have influenced numerous other people to take an interest in the environment.

Roderick Langmere Haig-Brown was born in February 1908 in England, but by the late 1920s he was travelling through Washington state and British Columbia, where he first became impassioned about environmental issues in general and sports fishing in particular. While passing through Seattle on one visit, he met his future wife, Ann Elmore. In 1934 the two were married and soon after moved to this house on the banks of the Campbell River. They called it "Above Tide," and it was their home until their respective deaths, Roderick in 1976 and Ann in 1990.

The property is best described in Haig-Brown's own words, in *Measure of the Year*:

The land we live on is a rough square of twenty acres, based on eight or nine hundred feet of river bank. A dusty gravel road divides the twenty acres, nine acres on the river side of the road, eleven acres on the other side. The house stands just about in the centre of the nine acres – over a hundred feet from the edge of the river.

Haig-Brown's study overlooked the lawn and a rose border which ran down to the river. It was the perfect setting for a writer who was enthralled with the outdoors.

Together Roderick and Ann Haig-Brown devoted their whole lives to the protection of B.C.'s rivers, particularly those on which wild salmon depend. Defending the Fraser River from hydroelectric dams was one of their most successful projects. Roderick also wrote about sports fishing and conservation: in all he wrote 25 natural-history and conservation books as well as many novels and essays. He also served as a county magistrate for the North Island and was very involved in his community.

~ 2250 Campbell River Road ~

As well as running the household and raising their four children, Ann Haig-Brown was active in her church and charitable organizations in the Campbell River area and supported her husband's conservation endeavours. A transition house in Campbell River is named after her.

On Saturday, October 9, 1976, which was Thanksgiving weekend that year, Roderick was working on his property as usual. He had stacked some wood and cut the grass with his new tractor by the time his wife called him in for lunch. As he walked below the window of his study, he collapsed and died.

Roderick Haig-Brown's wish had been for his property to be enjoyed by everyone after his death. One of his pet projects had been to restore Kingfisher Creek, which ran through his property, so that coho and cutthroat salmon could spawn there. The Haig-Brown Kingfisher Creek Society was formed after his death to complete the work of bringing the creek back to health.

Today, the original property is owned by the provincial government. The house and contents have been managed by the Campbell River Museum since the death of Ann Haig-Brown. Valerie Haig-Brown, also a writer, wrote *Deep Currents,* using her father's many records and research material to document her parents' lives and their home in Campbell River.

The Haig-Brown property was dedicated as an historic site in 1990. Today it serves as a resource centre, a museum, a bed and breakfast, and a seminar and workshop centre.

The beautiful Campbell River itself flows past the property, with Kingfisher Creek running nearby. This wonderful setting is ideal for learning more about natural history and fishing. The town of Campbell River hosts the Haig-Brown Festival in September every year with fly-fishing events, an antique book fair and a garden party at which regional foods are served.

Back in 1950, Roderick Haig-Brown wrote the following words in *Measure of the Year*, and they seem even more pertinent now:

I have been, all my life, what is known as a conservationist. It seems clear beyond possibility of argument that any given generation of men can have only a lease, not ownership, of the earth; and one essential term of the lease is that the earth be handed down on to the next generation with unimpaired potentialities. This is the conservationist's concern.

THE LITTLE RED HOUSE

From Float House to Airline Office

When Louise Betts Smith was a child during World War II she witnessed the arrival of a small floathouse, towed from Rough Bay on Malcolm Island to Port McNeill by two brothers, Noel and Babe Wilkinson. It would later become her family's home and for many years was known simply as "the little red house" in Port McNeill.

The house had begun its life on a float in Rough Bay, as a storage shed for fish. This storage space later became the living room and master bedroom of the house. Sawdust in the walls acted as insulation to keep the ice from melting so the fish would stay fresh until taken by the packers to nearby canneries.

Later the building was converted into a house and was owned by the O'Conner family of Port Hardy; they renovated and enlarged it to prepare for the arrival of relatives from Britain who were escaping wartime bombing. In exchange for raw logs, A. M. Wastell of Telegraph Cove supplied the O'Conners with enough finished lumber to expand the house. Money was scarce at that time and most people bartered goods rather than paying money. A back bedroom, bathroom, pantry and three upstairs bedrooms were all added to the little house, which was then sided with shingles.

Plans changed and the relatives never arrived, so the house was eventually sold to the Wilkinsons who floated it to Port McNeill where it still stands. The space cleared for the house was a lot between the site of the former Christenson family home (now the Sportsman Café) and the timekeeper's prefab house (where people now park their boat trailers). Its address today is 2001 Beach Drive.

The Wilkinson brothers were logging-truck operators contracting for the Pioneer Timber Company. As contractors they had to find accommodation for their families in Port McNeill, hence their decision to float the house there. Unfortunately all the ceilings in the little house were very low and the Wilkinson men were very tall! Nonetheless, for three years the two Wilkinson families managed to survive in the house together, even though Babe Wilkinson could stand up straight only in the centre of the upstairs rooms. During those three years they built a platform at the front door and levelled off the space between the house and the plank road in order to plant some grass and make a garden. They then put up a cedar picket fence to enclose the front yard.

148

~ 2001 Beach Drive ~

149

Meanwhile, the Betts family lived farther down the road in their small shack, which consisted of one bedroom and a kitchen. There were five in the family: Wallace and Janet Betts and their children, Sam, Gerry and Louise, the little girl who watched the arrival of the floathouse with childish wonder. A second daughter, Elizabeth, was born in 1950.

When the Wilkinsons decided to sell their house for $1,000 in 1946, Wallace Betts made an offer to buy it. By then, his wife had had more than enough of life in a shack and was tired of having to boil water to wash clothes in a tub with a scrub board alongside. (That same tub was also used for family bathing; many years later it was given to the Port Hardy Museum.) But Wallace Betts only had $500 and he asked Pioneer Timber if they would advance him the other $500 so he could buy the house. Once they agreed, the Betts family happily moved into the little red house.

For the next six decades, Janet Betts was considered a legend in Port McNeill. Born Janet Anderson in Kelowna in 1912, she and her family had moved to Function Junction near Whistler when she was still a child. Her father was killed in a railway accident and her mother remarried. The family was in the logging business and Janet's schooling was done by correspondence until grade four or five. She became an avid reader and instilled this love in her own children.

In 1937 she married Wallace Betts, a high school graduate from New Brunswick who had come west to log. In 1942 he took a job with Pioneer Timber in Port McNeill. She was thrilled to move to the little red house with her family because it was the first house she had ever lived in that had running water, indoor plumbing and electricity.

When the family moved in, Sam and Louise shared the back bedroom and Gerry was in a crib in his parents' room. After Elizabeth was born in 1950, Gerry moved upstairs to share a room with Sam. Louise then had a room with a dormer, and from her large window she could see from one end of the logging camp to the other. She loved it because she saw everything that happened in Port McNeill. She watched all the boats arriving or leaving the government dock and saw everyone travelling the road in front of their house.

The Betts purchased a washing machine and refrigerator first, great luxuries for Janet Betts. Eventually the old wood-burning cookstove, purchased from Eaton's in 1943, was also replaced, but Janet hated to part with the old one because it had also heated the house. When the firewall between the firebox and the oven burned through, Janet started searching for a similar new stove or replacements parts, but by then it was the late 1950s and wood-burning stoves were no longer being manufactured. Undaunted, Janet set about fixing the stove herself with pieces of steel fitted into the place where the firewall was burned. She then mixed sand, salt, ashes and water to make a paste, which she spread in the firebox. The mixture was replaced once a month. She had learned this trick from watching her mother fix their stoves in Whistler when their fireboxes had burned. Even though the Betts family eventually had a new electric range, Janet still insisted on having a wood heater placed beside it.

Janet also loved spending time in her garden, the space for which she had created by clearing bushes and cutting away brush. When the children came home from school she would start a bonfire to burn the debris, and they would roast potatoes on the fire. All the children in the neighbourhood joined in the fun until bedtime. Louise remembers having a fire as a highlight in those days, and whenever things became boring they would ask their mother if they could have another fire. There was always plenty of material to burn because all the land was cleared and dug by Janet Betts. She refused the use of a machine. While she was busy clearing the land, Wallace was digging out the ground for a septic tank, as well as building onto the front and back porches of the house, and adding a woodshed.

Janet's garden was soon full of vegetables and flowers. Once a bear ran through her honeysuckle and Janet rushed out in her shorts to chase him away. That same honeysuckle bush and some fuchsias were later moved, and both now grow in her son Gerry's garden in Port Alice.

Janet Betts and her husband were also very active in the community. Janet taught Sunday school, helped run a library, cleaned the community hall and helped in the parent-teacher association and the Girl Guides. Janet's passion for books encouraged her children to be great readers and they often referred to their home as "a book house." Books on all manner of subjects were everywhere.

Janet Betts was also a wonderful cook and often served meals to as many as 20 men from the mining camp at one time. There was nowhere in town to eat when they came back from the mine, so Janet's kitchen improvised as an instant restaurant. Her son described her as "a pit bull with a purpose" when something needed to be done. She didn't hesitate, but went right ahead and did it. At one time she successfully campaigned to have a railing built on the old government wharf.

Pioneer Timber Company houses were all painted red with green roofs and white trim, and the Betts painted theirs to match. The houses that once belonged to a Japanese company known as the Nippon Soda McNeill Trading Company were painted grey. This company was closed down by the government at the outbreak of World War II and then leased by the Pioneer Timber Company. The buildings and surrounding land were referred to always as "alien property." Eventually all those buildings were sold to Pioneer Timber, and the company president decided it would be better to paint all the grey houses and the red houses in pastel shades. Most adopted this colour scheme, but the Betts loved their red house and kept it that colour.

A wire fence was later built around the Betts' property to keep their dog in and unwanted people out. This fence certainly saved Janet Betts' garden when some cows crossed the Nimpkish River and came up from the beach looking for something tasty to eat. When the fence was first erected, someone hung a "Betts' Concentration Camp" sign on it. Despite this early attempt at graffiti that fence has stood for over 50 years. The posts were replaced as they rotted, but the wire is original.

When Port McNeill became a municipality, Wallace and Janet Betts bought the house from Pioneer Timber and then began paying taxes to the municipality. In 1987 Wallace passed away, but Janet remained in her little red house for another 12 years with her black Labrador, Babe, for company.

In 1999, Janet moved to the mainland to live out her remaining years near her daughter Louise. As they drove away from the house, she turned sadly for the last time and whispered, "Goodbye, little house." In August 2003, Port McNeill legend Janet Betts passed away at the age of 91, and a memorial service was held in September at the Port McNeill Community Hall. The little red house, with its many memories, is today a branch office for Pacific Eagle Aviation.

WESTERN FOREST PRODUCTS GUEST HOUSE

Alien Property in Port McNeill?

This is a story to commemorate not just one house, but many. Only one of them, however, still exists to remind us that in the 1930s a Japanese firm operated a logging business called the Nippon Soda McNeill Trading Company in Port McNeill.

The company built houses for their employees with families in what is now the commercial section of Port McNeill. Other buildings were bunkhouses for workers or offices. When World War II broke out, all these properties were expropriated by the government, and the Japanese people were sent to various camps throughout British Columbia.

The Japanese section of town was then known as "alien property," and the locals referred to this cluster of buildings as "Jap Town." After the Japanese left, Tommy and Amy Muir lived in the first house from the dock, and it was Tommy's job to look after all the alien property. The second house along the plank road was later lived in by the Russ Dickie family. Like all the others it was painted grey but, unlike them, it had been renovated from a bunkhouse into a house with a kitchen, living room and two bedrooms. The Dickie house is the only one still standing and is known today as the "Western Forest Products Guest House."

Some of the houses had large red circles painted on the walls, but the people who moved in quickly painted them over. The circles were the Japanese emblem of the rising sun and by 1943, when many Pioneer Timber Company employees were taking over the alien properties, Canada was at war with Japan, and people on the west coast feared an attack at any time. They wanted all traces of the Japanese who had once occupied these houses promptly removed.

Another of the houses was once the office for the Japanese logging company. It was not more than 500 square feet but would house a family of five. Bunk beds were built against the wall in one room for two children, and a curtain divided it from the double bed where the parents slept. Underneath the bed and at the foot of the bunks were storage places for flour, sugar and prunes. The other room housed a wood cookstove, a table, chairs and a cot, which was used as a couch or

~ WFP Guest House, Port McNeill ~

an extra bed if the family had company. A tap outside the house supplied the water, which was carried inside in a bucket as needed for washing and cooking. With no refrigeration inside, butter, vegetables and fruit were stored in a tight container outside in a shaded area.

Union Steamships and the Canadian Pacific Railway boats came to Port McNeill from Vancouver once or twice a week. Most families occupying the alien property ordered their groceries from Woodwards, and when the steamships arrived fresh meat was available. Stewing beef, sausages and chicken were canned and preserved for later use. Whenever ice cream arrived, it had to be eaten quickly because it could not be kept — ice-cream day became a special treat for the families.

Some of the houses had bathrooms but most did not. The Japanese toilets were back in the bush. Mostly they were small buildings about 6 by 12 feet, with a bar to sit on. Most of the children feared falling down the holes. This actually happened on one occasion and when the child in question was rescued and led home, his mother stripped him down and hosed him while everyone stood around watching.

In 1943 the Pioneer Timber Company had a Chinese road crew who built and maintained the plank logging roads. These roads looked rather like railroads. A plank road extended from the steamship dock to Jap Town, a name that was later replaced by China Town or sometimes even "Chink Town." The Chinese who lived on property owned by Pioneer Timber were often harassed by children, who threw rocks and chanted racist "chinky, chinky Chinamen" ditties. These children were equally unpleasant on occasion to the other white families who lived on the alien property.

The Japanese left behind a water tower about 20 feet high. It was there that the children of the neighbourhood gathered to play war games. Beside the water tower stood a small shack, which was believed to have once stored dynamite.

Eventually the shack, tower and toilets all disappeared because they were considered dangerous. The Japanese had also built a reservoir, but later the water for the settlers' camp came from Bear Creek. This water was usually muddy, so most people took containers down to the spring in the woods for their water supply.

Both the Pioneer Timber Company houses and those held by the public trustee after the Japanese were forced to leave had extraordinarily pretty gardens full of flowers. The Japanese had obviously set the standard, since they had been there first. Their flower beds were circular and most were filled with daffodils bulbs which bloom each spring, surrounded by pinks. There were also numerous forget-me-nots and English daisies. Even today many Port McNeill gardens have pinks, daisies, daffodils and forget-me-nots that originated in Japanese gardens six decades ago.

In the late 1940s the Koerner family bought Pioneer Timber. More houses were built or moved in beside the Japanese houses, some of which were moved away. A few of the houses were turned around so that they now faced the road that went down to the new government dock. Most of the houses were added to and renovated.

By 1966, when Port McNeill was incorporated as a municipality, the main part of town had started to move up the hill, and the sites of the old Nippon Soda McNeill Trading Company and the Pioneer Timber Company camps became the commercial district. Some of the old houses were moved up the hill; others were put on floats and moved to Hyde Creek and other locations.

The last piece of alien property, the Dickie House, is the only one remaining in the spot where it was built. The road in front is now paved; the old plank roads have long since disappeared. Today, as a guest house, the old Dickie house is the only reminder of that unhappy era in the 1940s when the world was at war and the Japanese were considered the enemy.

WASTELL MANOR

From Lean-to Shack to Boardwalk Hotel

Telegraph Cove on the northeast coast of Vancouver Island was named in 1911 by A. M. Wastell, after the government set up a telegraph station there. At that time Mr. Wastell was the manager of the sawmill and box factory for B.C. Fishing and Packing in Alert Bay, across the water. He also owned the standing timber at Telegraph Cove and soon began to log that area. Logging came to a halt during World War I, but in 1918 the logging camp returned to the cove and remained there until 1922.

Wastell had always envisioned a great future for the cove, so that same year he set up a saltery with some Japanese partners. He also purchased a sawmill to make wooden boxes for shipping the salted salmon to Japan. He floated the mill over from Sointula on Malcolm Island in 1922. After three years, however, the saltery began to lose money and had to close down, and with no further need for fish boxes, the sawmill also closed. The sawmill at Alert Bay was closed in 1928 when a change was made from wooden to cardboard fish boxes for transportation.

Meanwhile Wastell had asked his son, Fred, if he would be interested in moving to Telegraph Cove. Fred was newly married and out of work, so he took up the offer and reopened the sawmill at Telegraph Cove. He

and his long-time friend, Alex McDonald, became partners. Together they slowly rebuilt the sawmill so that it was supplying lumber again for boats, buildings, docks, bridges and logging railways on the North Island. With the sawmill prospering, it was not long before a small village with as many as 60 permanent residents grew up in Telegraph Cove.

The house known as Wastell Manor today became Fred Wastell's home in 1929. It had originally been a 12- by 14-foot lean-to shack occupied by the bookkeeper at the saltery. The shack was empty when Fred arrived so he moved in and began renovating. He raised the main part of the house to create more space for his family. The sunroom was added in 1980 to take advantage of the exceptional views. Fred and his family lived in Telegraph Cove for almost 50 years. The well-known camp tender that Fred once owned, called *Gikumi*, is used today for whale-watching trips, offered by its current owner, Jim Borrowman.

In 1979 Gordie and Marilyn Graham of Port Alice offered to lease the property at Telegraph Cove to build a campground and to develop a marina in the bay. The idea was encouraged because it was obvious by then that

~ Boardwalk, Telegraph Cove ~

the future of the little cove lay in tourism, rather than logging or fishing.

The sawmill ran until 1984 under the management of Ken Curry, but eventually it was no longer profitable. The campground and marina opened in 1980 and the Grahams maintained all the houses and the boardwalk until 1988.

That year Lot 79 (the Wastell property) was purchased by Dave Bilinski who, at the same time, agreed to sell the whole village and campground area to Telegraph Cove Resorts, a company owned by Gordie Graham and Jim Findlay. Bilinski logged some of the acreage, but made sure that wooded areas around the cove and campground area were left untouched. In 1989 the undeveloped property owned by Bilinski was purchased by Jim Findlay, who then formed a company with Bud Wagner to further develop this property.

Wastell House, located on the boardwalk, was turned into a five-room hotel in 1998. Today it is furnished to reflect its era and is one of the delightful buildings that make up the village of Telegraph Cove.

The history of Telegraph Cove, with its sawmill and saltery, has been retained, though the sheltered cove has also adapted to the needs of the tourist industry. Visitors can enjoy the bygone era in places such as Wastell Manor, while also experiencing the thoroughly modern pastime of whale-watching in nearby waters.

BURTON HOUSE

Cookhouse, Barracks and Family Home

The Burton House at Telegraph Cove was built in 1929, the same year as the Wastell house. However, the balloon style of construction was used to build it. This means there is no frame and the outside wallboards support the roof — if the roof were removed for any reason, the walls would collapse!

In the beginning the little house served as a cookhouse for the workers at Telegraph Cove, and during World War II, it became a barracks for military use. From 1947 until 1985, however, the house was home to Jimmy and Thelma Burton. A second peak roof was added over the original roof in 1947 when the Burtons moved in.

Thelma originally came to the cove to act as nanny for Fred Wastell's daughters. One of those daughters, Pat Wastell Norris, is the author of a history of Telegraph Cove, *Time & Tide*. Thelma met Jimmy Burton there and the two were soon married, their wedding taking place in Vancouver. Moving back to Telegraph Cove, Thelma later became postmistress there and ran the general store for many years. The building that housed the old post office and store was built in 1951 by Lawrie Creelman of the Alert Bay Pile Driving Company.

The Burton House was always known for its beautiful window boxes, which Thelma kept filled with colourful begonias. Today, like many other houses on the boardwalk, it is used for tourist accommodation. The Burtons have retired to Comox, but their memories of their old Telegraph Cove home are happy ones. Thelma Burton recalls, however, that the house was always hard to heat. The fuel they used was mostly sawdust in the beginning, but later things improved for them financially and they burned oil.

A persistent low-lying fog and constant dampness imparted an eerie aspect to life on the North Island, but communal life was always warm among the residents of Telegraph Cove. For instance, Alex McDonald (friend and partner of Fred Wastell) and his wife Mary resided in what was once "the Floating Hospital," a building that had slipped off its barge on its way to Pender Harbour and was towed into Telegraph Cove in 1930. Alex and Mary lived there for many years and Mary was known as "Auntie Mary" to all the children of the cove because of the delicious cookies she always had ready for them.

Nearby is the old mess hall used by the airforce during World War II. The mill was turned to war work and airmen were employed to cut lumber to build more

~ Boardwalk, Telegraph Cove ~

161

bases up the coast at Port Hardy, Coal Harbour and Bella Bella. After the war, the mess hall became a cookhouse, and in the 1950s it was the cove's community hall, where Friday-night movies were shown and Saturday-night dances held. In 1975 this building was converted into apartments.

In the 1930s, many Japanese-Canadians resided at the cove and their homes are still there. The Okura House belonged to a Japanese millwright. The Nakamura House (built in 1931) was the home of the owner of many seine boats that supplied fish to the saltery. The mill's caretaker, Mr. Ogawa, also built his house in 1931 and made fish boxes for the salted salmon. After the Japanese were interned at the beginning of World War II, Mr. Ogawa's house was used by sawmill employees.

The old schoolhouse, built in 1931, completes the village that Thelma and Jim Burton enjoyed for so many years. This building was the original school, but it closed down while the airforce occupied the cove. It was then the residence of Major McAffery, but reverted to a school again after the war until 1956, when the Kokish school opened, at which time it once more became a private residence. From 1959 until 1989 the Ziggiotti family lived there, but it is now the summer residence of Gordie and Marilyn Graham.

The charming boardwalk village at the cove has many other buildings, including the freight shed used today as the office of Stubbs Island Charters; the 1940 millwright house built by Fred Wastell's uncle; the food-storage shed (*circa* 1940) that today houses the Seymour Gallery; and the old bunkhouse that is now a duplex. More recently built houses include the 1962 Farrant house, whose owners have lived in the cove since 1966, the 1965 Vinderskov house and the renovated Crouter house.

A special air of comradeship and memories from days gone by still linger at Telegraph Cove, making it worthy of a visit.

FINAL WORD

In *If More Walls Could Talk,* I have tried again to include all varieties, sizes and designs of heritage houses, this time throughout Vancouver Island. I have been amazed at the diversity I found as I travelled the island. From miners' cottages to Maclure mansions, I have covered a wide spectrum of establishments, enabling the reader to capture a glimpse of what life must have been like in those homes throughout the decades since they were built, spanning the years from the 1850s to the 1940s. As always, Lynn's illustrations add an incredible authenticity to the descriptions of these buildings.

The preservation of these heritage houses is a constant, ongoing project, one that most of the current owners are ready to tackle with enthusiasm. Meanwhile, I feel that we are merely scratching the surface of this topic, and that there are many more heritage-house stories still to be told. In that regard, my inquisitive writer's mind is continually searching for more tales that are worth recording for future generations to enjoy.

"Science is built up with facts, as a house is with stones. But a collection of facts is no more a science than a heap of stones is a house," wrote Jules-Henri Poincare in *La Science et l'Hypothese.*

It is true that there is a great deal more to the evolution of a house than merely the wood, bricks and mortar with which it was built, or later renovated. The real story of a house's heritage concerns the inhabitants who were born, lived, loved or died within its walls.

BIBLIOGRAPHY

Barr, Jennifer Nell. *Saanich Heritage Structures: An Inventory.* The Corporation of the District of Saanich, Victoria, B.C., 1991.

Cadwaladr, Margaret. *In Veronica's Garden.* Madrona Books & Publishing, Qualicum Beach, B.C., 2002.

Carr, Emily. *The Book of Small.* Irwin Publishing, Toronto, Ont., 1942.

Green, Valerie. *If These Walls Could Talk: Victoria's Houses From The Past.* TouchWood Editions, Victoria, B.C., 2001.

Gregson, Harry. *A History of Victoria, 1842 – 1970.* Victoria Observer Publishing Co. Ltd., Victoria, B.C., 1970.

Haig-Brown, Valerie. *Deep Currents.* Orca Book Publishers, Victoria, B.C., 1997.

Harrison, Eunice M. L. *The Judge's Wife: Memoirs of a British Columbia Pioneer.* Ronsdale Press, Vancouver, B.C., 2002.

Haig-Brown, Roderick L. *Measure of the Year.* Essay Index Reprint Series, Ayer Co. Publishers, Vancouver, B.C., 1950.

Isenor, D. E., W. N. McInnis, E. G. Stephens, and D. E. Watson. *Land of Plenty: A History of the Comox District.* Ptarmigan Press, Campbell River, B.C., 1987.

Johnson, P. M. *Nanaimo: A Short History.* Trendex Publications & Western Heritage, Nanaimo, B.C., 1974.

Lillard, Charles. *Seven Shillings a Year: The History of Vancouver Island.* Horsdal & Schubart Ltd., Ganges, B.C., 1986.

Mitchell, Helen A. *Diamond in the Rough — A History of Campbell River.* Campbell River, B.C., 1966.

Nanaimo Community Heritage Commission. *Columns, Cornices & Coal: The Heritage Resources of Nanaimo.* Nanaimo Community Heritage Commission, Nanaimo, B.C., 1999.

Norcross, Blanche E. *Nanaimo Retrospective — The First Century.* Nanaimo Historical Society, Nanaimo, B.C., 1979.

Norris, Pat Wastell. *Time & Tide: A History of Telegraph Cove.* Harbour Publishing Co. Ltd., Madeira Park, B.C., 1995.

Segger, Martin. *The Buildings of Samuel Maclure.* Sono Nis Press, Victoria, B.C., 1986.

Segger, Martin and Douglas Franklin. *Exploring Victoria's Architecture.* Sono Nis Press, Victoria, B.C., 1996.

Wylie, Brad. *Qualicum Beach: A History of Vancouver Island's Best-Kept Secrets.* B. Wylie, Qualicum Beach, B.C., 1992.

INDEX

Valerie Green is the author of several books on Victoria's past, including *If These Walls Could Talk*; *Above Stairs*: *Social Life in Upper-Class Victoria*; *No Ordinary People*: *Victoria's Mayors Since 1862;* and *Upstarts and Outcasts*: *Victoria's Not-So-Proper Past*.

Lynn Gordon-Findlay is an intern associate with the Architectural Institute of British Columbia. She works mainly in pencil, pen-and-ink and watercolour; she has provided illustrations for Valerie's newspaper columns on Victoria's heritage buildings.